Enjoy

California! by *Camaro*

The great food and wine adventure (at low cost)

- Hidden Restaurants: Northern California
- Hidden Restaurants: Southern California
- Little Restaurants of San Francisco
- Little Restaurants of Los Angeles
- Little Restaurants of San Diego
- Wine Tasting in California: A Free Weekend
- L. A. On Foot: A Free Afternoon

Perhaps the most beautifully illustrated books in the Western World. Glove compartment size, and only $1.95.

At your favorite bookstore, or by mail from the publisher. See back of book for order information.

★★★★★ A Camaro Five Star Guide

Sketches by David Yeadon

The Little Restaurants of San Francisco

By Roz Lewis
Joe Pierce

Camaro Publishing Co.
LOS ANGELES—SAN FRANCISCO

Library of Congress Catalog Number: 73-85631
ISBN 0-913290-06-8

CAMARO PUBLISHING COMPANY
LOS ANGELES, CALIFORNIA 90009

Contents

The following list attempts to categorize restaurants according to their specialties. There are two conglomerate categories: "All-American" and "Miscellaneous." An "All-American" classification doesn't mean a restaurant necessarily serves strictly Yankee pot roast. It means that you will probably be familiar with the majority of the dishes available. A "Miscellaneous" restaurant means we just didn't know exactly what to call it. The other divisions I think will be self-explanatory, but if you can't tell whether or not a restaurant offers what you're looking for, call them and ask.

Introduction

If an iceberg flattened the hills of San Francisco, centuries from now archaeologists would unearth frozen food better than the Jolly Green Giant ever thought possible in his wildest ho-ho-ho's. Since this particular catastrophe seems unlikely, and frozen food usually isn't worth defrosting anyway, we've written a guide to the ups and downs of San Francisco dining as it now exists (earthquakes notwithstanding).

Why did we decide to write a guide to dining out in the Bay Area? Number one, most people aren't aware of the wealth of good, hidden restaurants available to them at low cost. Number two, even that cute little place down the block may not be very good, so why chance a wasted evening and a deflated wallet. On the other hand, if a friend recommends a restaurant, you're not taking such a chance, and you may even experience some exciting dining adventures.

This train of thought led us to write this book the way we have—as if we were recommending these delightful spots to our friends.

We took advantage of the compactness of the city and combed the hills and alleys looking for dining hideaways. We even surprised ourselves with the number of good restaurants we found out of the hundreds we tried.

Since different sections of town often are just a few blocks square, we also found you could dine on a different type of cuisine each night of the week and never be very far from a completely different and delicious dining experience. For example, from downtown to Chinatown to North Beach to Fisherman's Wharf, is a straight line through some fascinating gastronomic territory.

Other restaurant guides seemed to miss the point. Maybe the restaurants they listed ranged in price from the sublime to the ridiculous. Maybe they told us too much about a restaurant's history and not enough about its present. Maybe their entire perspective on dining out was somewhat out of alignment with ours. Maybe they just hadn't checked out their places for a few years—and anyone's milk could have curdled in that time. Most importantly, maybe they weren't up to date on prices. And the rise in the cost of food has dated many guides very quickly. A place that charged $3.50 for dinner less than three years ago could be charging $7.50 now. Since we're all concerned with what we spend for dinner, this was a major consideration in our deciding to write a new guide to dining out inexpensively in San Francisco.

So we compiled a list of all the things we didn't like about other guides and added a few notes about what we ourselves would want to know before venturing forth to a new restaurant.

What we hope we've ended up with is a guide oriented toward low-priced, relatively unknown restaurants that can be enjoyed by everyone looking for a dining adventure at inflation fighting prices. We also threw in a few restaurants you've probably heard of—but might have been wondering whether or not to try. Actually some very popular places are popular for good cause, and shouldn't be missed just because everybody already knows about them. We also realized that, while dining out on a budget is the ideal course (followed by your choice of soup or salad), there are occasions when we all feel like a splurge. A splurge doesn't mean just paying a premium for cloth napkins and spotless drinking glasses. It means getting your money's worth in all areas: food, atmosphere and service. The splurges we've included are well worth the prices they charge.

We are not saying that our judgment about dining out is any better than yours. We didn't come from gourmet environments (I guess that's why paté has always been chopped liver to us) and we didn't have any special training. We simply judge food by how it tastes and how it looks. If the ingredients are not traditional or the preparation is unorthodox, these factors are unimportant: it's the result that counts with us. (Of course, if we ordered veal scallopini, we weren't happy with veal parmesan.) In fact, we greatly value food that has been prepared imaginatively. An interesting dollop of this or garnish of that can make a dish special if it enhances the overall flavor or appearance. Appearance may seem secondary, but even the most delicious creation will be unappreciated if its presentation is unappetizing.

The recommendations we make, therefore, are obviously based on *our* tastebuds. When we tried a restaurant, we let everyone in our party taste all the dishes and then took a consensus. Many people fight the urge to taste someone else's dinner. This is foolish—unless, of course, they don't want to relinquish a taste of their own or they don't know the person whose dinner they're coveting. If we all agreed that a dish was good, that was fine. But the main question always was—would we come back for it? Not, would we come back if somebody gave us a free pass, but would we make an effort to return? If our decision was "yes," it seemed likely that yours might be, too.

Since we were most interested in inexpensive dining out (we looked mainly for restaurants where dinners can be had for less than $5 per person), we judged a restaurant first of all by its food. Anybody can provide a low priced meal, but a *good* low priced meal is an oasis. Also, since low prices on the menu usually reflect a lack of high expenditure on overhead, atmosphere was a plus—any atmosphere.

Atmosphere turned out to be a difficult factor to judge. Some people think that a restaurant

seating 500 with red and black plastic everything
has atmosphere. Others feel that atmosphere consists of eating among the neighborhood crowd,
with foreign languages resounding in their ears.
One important point to remember when dining out
inexpensively, however, is that the extra money
you're *not* paying for the meal has to be reflected
somewhere. Usually this means that the restaurant's
decor will never be featured in *House Beautiful.*
It may also mean paper napkins, unclothed tables,
a bare floor, a cracked ceiling and hand-printed
menus.

Our comments about service, on the other hand,
do not reflect the prices on the menu, but rather
the attitude of the restaurant's staff. A high priced
waiter often acts as if he's doing you a favor by
simply casting his shadow on your dinner plate.
A low-priced waiter may figure that if you're dining
inexpensively, the tip probably won't be too
generous—so why bother? Somewhere in between
is the waiter who does his best to make your meal
satisfactory. This is the kind we looked for—and
found surprisingly often in many places throughout
the city.

Just as a surly or inattentive waiter can ruin a
good meal, a special waiter is to be cherished. So
there's no harm in asking for him when you go to
a restaurant, or just sitting in his section if you seat
yourself. And in most of the restaurants described
in this book, seating yourself is the obvious course
of action—otherwise, the management will think
you want to eat standing up in the doorway. If the
service is good (and a slow kitchen is not the waiter's

fault), we believe that the waiter should be suitably rewarded. A standard tip is usually 15 percent of the total bill. For excellent service, 20 percent is appropriate. We will not tell you to never withhold a tip because we, too, have encountered our share of incompetents. But before taking such a drastic measure, make sure the problem was the waiter's fault. If you are less than satisfied with the service— whether or not you decide to leave a tip—please tell someone in the restaurant the reason for your unhappiness so that the problem can be remedied.

Many of the little places in this book note on their menus that certain items require a long time to prepare, so you can decide whether or not you want to put up with a wait. If a place is exceedingly busy, you may also have to wait a little longer than usual to get your dinner. If service is simply slower than normal on a specific evening, the waiter should warn you. Of course, extremely quick service can also be inconvenient, and may mean that the entree was simply warmed rather than prepared individually

While we were doing our test dining, we never told anyone in any of the hundreds of restaurants we tried what we were doing. Even after we had decided to include a restaurant in the book, we didn't identify ourselves because we did not want to lose our anonymity when we returned. We wanted to make sure that the food and service we received would be no better than anyone else could expect.

Now that we've established what we looked for and how we looked, let us tell you what we found. We found more good Italian, Chinese and seafood

restaurants than we thought possible in one city. We
found neighborhoods with so many good dining
spots that this factor alone should raise local property
values. We found a conspicuous lack of inexpensive
steak restaurants and not one decent barbecue house.
This doesn't mean that these places don't exist, but
only that we didn't find them. And this last point is
important: no restaurant guide on the Bay Area can
be definitive. The places we found were suggested
to us by friends (many of whom gave up their secrets
very reluctantly) or were discovered simply by continuously driving around. If your favorite restaurant
isn't here, we probably didn't know about it. Possibly
the prices were too high. Or maybe we ate there and
didn't like it. Restaurants have their off nights just
like people.

Starting a restaurant is a much easier proposition
than keeping one open. So if you find a restaurant
that you're really fond of, support it and tell your
friends about it. We'd be the last ones to tell you
to keep going to the same old place, but don't
neglect your favorites either. If one of them closes
its doors permanently, it may be because it simply
can't afford to stay open any longer for the few
people who want to keep it their little secret.

Hopefully, by now you're interested in sharing
the results of our dining-out adventures. If we've
enticed you, you can continue exploring on your
own. But do explore. Don't just stay within the
city limits. We've included some gems we found in
Marin County, and there's no reason you shouldn't
look there, too. We've told you about good places
in Pacifica, in Princeton-by-the-Sea, even in South

City and even in East Bay. So go exploring. When you spot a restaurant that looks interesting, ask to see the menu before you sit down. This will not only help you decide whether or not it offers anything you like, but will also warn you ahead of time what size bill to expect.

We can't guarantee that since we went to press, prices haven't escalated, owners haven't changed or chefs haven't developed allergies to salt. The odds are that some minor catastrophes will have occured. If so, just turn the page and try again. The best way to make sure that a restaurant is still standing is to call before you go. Ask for whatever information you want to verify. It would be a shame to have had your heart set on Charlie's cheesecake only to discover that Charlie only bakes it on his mother's birthday, which was last week.

My thanks go to all those good souls with brave stomachs who helped us taste our way around the city: my husband Ritch, Bill and Lila Daniels, Kathy Pancoast, Steve Toms, Lee Berrigan, Barbara Klutinis, Judy and Paul Fayollat, Susan Wichman and of course the ever-ravenous Garth and Trish. Without their help, I would have definitely lost my anonymity (not to mention my figure) by being the only person in a restaurant eating four meals simultaneously. Of course that probably would have qualified me for the old Ed Sullivan show.

May we help you keep both your wallet and your stomach full.

Roz Lewis
San Francisco, California

Notes

Here is our somewhat ambiguous—but, we think, helpful—code to restaurant details.

Days and hours open: A restaurant may not serve meals continuously from the time it opens to the time it closes. If you are planning a particularly early or late dinner, check with the restaurant to find out the kitchen hours.

Availability of alcoholic beverages: Most restaurants offer something stronger than coffee to accompany your meal. But many don't. Others are limited to beer and wine. Since many people don't like to eat without drinking, we've noted exactly what beverages each restaurant serves. If we say "full bar," that usually means there is also a wine list.

Credit cards: A restaurant has to pay a percentage of the bill to the credit-card company if it accepts a card. For this reason, many restaurants will not accept any credit cards at all. If we say "all major credit cards accepted," we mean the five which appear below.

AE	American Express
BA	Bankamericard
CB	Carte Blanche
DC	Diners Club
MC	Master Charge

Reservations: Since not having a reservation when you need one can ruin an evening out, we have noted three types of situations where reservations should be considered. "Reservations essential" means you'll never get seated without them. "Reservations advisable" means it's a good idea to make them unless you don't mind waiting. "No reservations taken" means first come, first served.

About the Authors

ROZ LEWIS, a native Californian and UCLA graduate, has been a restaurant writer for over four years. By paying for all meals herself, and remaining anonymous to the restauranteurs, Roz has provided San Francisco perhaps the most objective and quality low-cost dining guide yet written.

JOE PIERCE, a native Kansan, and now a long time Bay Area and San Francisco Telegraph Hill resident has had a love of food and wine since college days some five years ago. He applied his studies in psychology plus a Masters degree to ferreting out the best little places in the City. His year's quest involved following leads provided by life-long residents and friends, where they dine at low cost, and where the chef's love of food and satisfying the customers palate seems to be more important than high prices and high profits.

Bill's Place

The next time you have a craving for a home-made hamburger but don't feel like making it at home, stop in at Bill's Place. It's the only spot in the neighborhood that shows signs of life during the day, and the signs are that everyone's hungry. Not hungry for a three-course meal, but basic hungry. Hamburger, chili and french fries hungry.

Hamburgers here are lean, flavorful and juicy. Hot dogs are looong and come with lots of goo, including tomatoes. The chili is hearty, but not too spicy, and the french fries are chunky and crispy.

There are two areas in which to dine: the restaurant itself, with its small tables and counter, and the "Friendly Garden" in back. The garden is the obvious choice when the weather permits; a lot of effort has been put into making it comfortable and attractive, and it is less crowded and noisy than the main dining area. But since this really isn't a place you go for atmosphere, even sitting at the counter is a good way to sample Bill's fare.

Because of its popularity, Bill's Place is often crowded. Fortunately, this doesn't seem to affect the food—though, at crowded times, don't expect a smile from your waitress.

2315 Clement St., San Francisco; (415) 221-5262
Daily 11:30 - 9:00
No bar
No credit cards
Reservations advisable

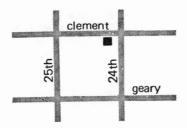

Delancey Street

Delancey Street sounds like the title of a 1944 musical starring Mickey Rooney. Far from it, Delancey Street is a delightful restaurant run by the Delancey Street drug rehabilitation program—successfully, we hope. Other than recommending the restaurant in order to support the worthy program, we can honestly praise its good food, excellent service and warm atmosphere. And in the high-priced neighborhood of Union Street, a $3.50 family-style dinner with a "bottomless" soup tureen is indeed a treasure.

For dinner, you are usually given a choice of four entrees (from such typical items as fried chicken, trout and spaghetti). A tureen of home-made soup (we enjoyed a mild but tasty clam chowder) is followed by a crisp lettuce-and-tomato salad served with cupfuls of dressing; then comes the entree, accompanied by vegetables (we had bacon-flavored green beans and rice with peas); finally you are presented with a basket of fresh fruit and a slice of cheese. The food is nicely prepared and the servings are more than adequate.

You can dine indoors by the big stove that keeps the huge kettle of soup warm, in an enclosed patio surrounded by white latticework and hanging plants, or on the open patio where you can watch the parade on Union Street from a delicious vantage point.

2032 Union St., San Francisco; (415) 346-9555
Tues. - Sun. 11:30 - 9:30; closed Mon.
Beer & wine
AE, BA, MC
Reservations advisable

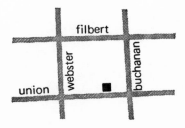

Neon Chicken

At first, when we heard people talking about the Neon Chicken, we were sure it was a new rock band.

Wrong again. It's a small, informal restaurant with the outline of a neon chicken in the window. And the only chicken dish it serves is its special Neon Chicken, cooked in red wine and mushroom sauce. It looks like more than half a chicken on the plate. So be hungry.

Other menu items include a terrific red snapper, beef tips in wine and mushroom sauce and daily specials. Of the specials, the stuffed pork chops are outstanding. Dinners include French bread and butter soup, salad and fresh vegetables. Dessert is extra, but worth it. Definitely order the house wine, which is Mondavi—an incredible selection for a house offerin

4063 18th St., San Francisco; (415) 863-0484
Daily 6 - 11
Beer & wine
MC
Reservations advisable

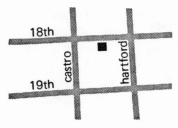

Pam Pam East

If you really enjoy live theater and occasionally attend some of the excellent shows in San Francisco's theater district, you're probably familiar with the lack of post-theater dining spots in the neighborhood. So if you're craving anything from a hamburger to a steak over which to discuss the evening's performance, try Pam Pam East. It's open 24 hours a day, so you'll even have time for two or three standing ovations before satisfying your appetite. You may have to wait to be seated, but the surrounding is pleasant and the decor is tastefully done with hanging ferns, used brick walls, posters and old-fashioned artifacts.

Pam Pam East is a restaurant - coffee shop combination, and the menu reflects this. You can eat breakfast, a sandwich or a full dinner any time of day or night. The hamburgers are excellent (especially the patty melt) and the steak teriyaki is also very good. An interesting special of the house is the steak soup, which is a cream soup with ground beef saute, tomatoes, carrots and celery. If you order a complete dinner, we recommend you have this instead of the rather ordinary dinner salad.

While the restaurant is generally crowded, the atmosphere is quiet and relaxed. Unfortunately, the rush is sometimes evident in the presentation of the food. However, the service is adequate and does not detract from your enjoyment of your meal.

398 Geary St., San Francisco; (415) 433-0113
Daily 24 hours
Full bar
No credit cards
Reservations advisable

PamPam east

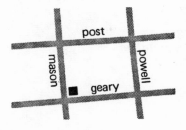

Perry's

Little out-of-the-way discoveries are nice most of the time. But occasionally you want to go to a place to "be seen" or to see all those famous people who supposedly go there to see each other. If the place also serves outstanding drinks and great food—well you can always say you were starving and just happened to be in the neighborhood. (This only works if the person to whom you're explaining doesn't realize that there are a dozen other places nearby into which you could have dropped.)

If you find yourself in such a mood, do try Perry's, because the food really is good. Everything from eggs Blackstone for breakfast (poached eggs served with real bacon bits, tomato and hollandaise sauce on a toasted English muffin) to Perry's mouth-watering hamburgers, served with homemade potato chips, is delicious. You can dine indoors in the old-fashioned saloon (complete with gleaming brass railings) or outdoors on the front or back patios. The interior is attractively done in 1890s style, and customers here really do seem to have that flamboyant spirit we associate with that decade.

If you like fun places and promise not to be disappointed if you don't get somebody's autograph, you'll really enjoy Perry's.

1944 Union St., San Francisco; (415) 922-9022
Daily 11:30 - 11
Full bar
AE, BA, MC
No reservations taken

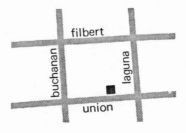

The Reunion

The Reunion was less than a year old when we stopped by, and located on a street where gastronomic competition is pretty rough. We hope it will see many future birthdays, for it offers excellent food at reasonable prices and an atmosphere especially enticing to jazz fans. Starting at about 9 p.m., Tuesday through Sunday, owner Tony Lewis and his trio emit jazz sounds that will spark your imagination. And if you've dined here first (dinner is served only until the entertainment begins), we can assure you of a totally enjoyable evening.

Complete dinners include soup, salad, bread, dessert and coffee or tea, and all bear such musical titles as Song of India (curried shrimp), Honeysuckle Rose (ravioli) and Body and Soul (burgundy stew). One of the finest selections is the Blue Flame—a London broil cooked to perfection and delicately charred.

In our society, we often equate price with quality. At the Reunion, prices, food and entertainment all reflect the image of a restaurant offering something special for the appreciative diner.

1969 Union St., San Francisco; (415) 346-3248
Daily 11:30 - 9
Full bar
No credit cards
No reservations taken

REUNION

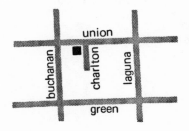

U.S. Restaurant

The U.S. Restaurant is *very* informal and *very* inexpensive. It is also generally *very* crowded, with a line made up of the diverse inhabitants of North Beach extending out onto the street. You may even end up sharing your wooden table with a local whose main interest is the roast beef dinner. You certainly won't have to worry about being underdressed, because even your blue jeans and T-shirt will fit in well with the unshaded fluorescent lights, linoleum floors and bland green walls.

But don't let the lack of decor discourage you. Especially if you're hungry. Entrees, including such basics as stew, roast beef, chicken and veal, are served with delicious green vegetables. If you supplement the main course with the "small" dinner salad of lettuce and tomatoes, you'll have a complete and filling meal. Or you may want to try the minestrone soup. Our only warning is to stay away from the ravioli, which seem too doughy.

The weekday specials are particularly good bargains. Don't be surprised if they run out of these—particularly the baked lasagne on Sunday. The U.S. Restaurant's cheeseburger is also a good bet—and so enormous that it's all you'll need to fill up.

431 Columbus Ave., San Francisco; (415) 362-6251
Tues. - Sun. 10 - 8; closed Mon.
Beer & wine
No credit cards
No reservations taken

Basque Hotel

One of San Francisco's best-known family dining spots, the Basque Hotel restaurant has managed for years to serve an incredible amount of good food at prices that defy inflation. And the hotel residents actually dine here. So between the Bay Area regulars and the boarders, you can usually expect a crowd. In fact, on Saturday nights you'd think the hotel was hosting a convention.

Everything is served family-style in big bowls or on platters that are passed down the table. There is no menu (just like home), so you take what they give you. And what they give you usually includes two meat entrees, soup, salad, two vegetables, bread, wine, dessert and coffee.

Obviously, if the food is passed along, so is a lot of the conversation. The atmosphere is very informal, and at tables seating between five and forty people, you know it's also apt to be rather loud. We suggest that you pretend you're attending a family reunion with people you haven't seen for ten years. That means they're not really strangers (so you can relax), and they're not really friends (so you have to get acquainted).

15 Romolo Place, San Francisco; (415) 398-1359
Tues. - Sun. 5 - 9; closed Mon.
Beer & wine
No credit cards
Reservations advisable

Chih Chiang

This is worth a special trip to the East Bay. Need I say more?

The menu offers a wide assortment of Northern Chinese dishes, and your waiter will probably make some very good suggestions as to what to order. Of the dishes we tried, shrimp with Szechuan sauce was our favorite. It includes many small, tender shrimp in a sauce that must be tasted in order to be described. Another especially good dish is the Northern-style pork, which consists of tender pieces of pork, cashews, scallions, bamboo shoots and delicious seasonings. For dessert, we tried the spun-sugar banana bits—bananas fried in a sugary batter, then dipped in ice water in order to solidify the coating. The result is scrumptious and light enough to top off the meal without placing an extra burden on an already satisfied stomach.

Chih Chiang has a rather elaborate facade and a tasteful, but simple, interior. Unfortunately, you should plan everything you want to order according to the breadth of your pocketbook, for it is easy to spend a lot here. If you want to make sure you don't overdo it, stick to the combination dinners.

5500 College Ave., Oakland; (415) 655-5677
Tues. - Sun. 11:30 - 9:30; closed Mon.
Beer & wine
BA
Reservations advisable

Chung King

Most people who enjoy Mandarin food like it because it is spicier than Cantonese. Well, at Chung King, you'd better ask for a pitcher of water on the side if you order Mandarin dishes. This stuff is hot!

The Chung King restaurant is simply but nicely decorated with red brick walls, wood paneling and Chinese prints and plants. The wooden tables are all cloth-covered and most are small and square, seating four people. However, in the center of the room are several large round tables, each with a lazy-susan contraption on top that turns, thus allowing everyone to get to everything without sticking his elbow in someone's eye. Our favorites of the *a la carte* dishes include mushee pork with pancakes (the pancakes are extra), twice-cooked pork (watch out for those little dry peppers), Mandarin beef and braised prawns in Szechuan sauce.

In the evening, there are candles on the tables and this can be a romantic spot. It is also a good place to try for lunch.

606 Jackson St., San Francisco; (415) 986-3899
Daily 11:30 - 10:00
Beer only
BA, MC
Reservations advisable

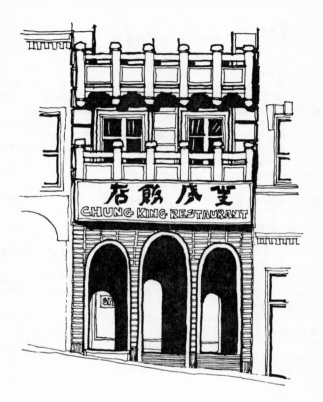

Far East Cafe

This is a very unusual place—nondescript on the outside and absolutely haunting on the inside. Beyond a huge archway are rows of curtained mahogany dining booths furnished with small, kitchen-type tables. Once inside a booth, with the curtain closed, the only places you can look are across the table and up. Assuming that you are already familiar with your dining partner, we suggest that you lift your eyes toward the two-story-high ceiling and concentrate on the massive lanterns that were brought over from China more than 50 years ago. The total atmosphere is one of clandestine meetings and secret plans—flavored with the faint aroma of soy sauce.

If you press the buzzer in your booth, a venerable waiter will appear and the decisions will begin. Both family-style dinners and *a la carte* dinners are available. Whichever you choose, try the fried egg rolls. They are enormous—about the size of frozen-orange juice cans, except that their contents are much more exotic and more delicious than you can imagine. The portions served on all the dishes are more than generous, and the variety is seemingly endless. One other notable feature is that the chow mein dishes come with your choice of crisp or soft noodles and are not vegetable-heavy. In fact, a chow mein ordered with soft noodles seems almost like an Oriental spaghetti.

Chinatown has its own special mystique, and the Far East Cafe really encourages you to delve into it.

631 Grant Ave., San Francisco; (415) 982-3245
Thurs. - Tues. noon - 11:00; closed Wed.
Full bar
No credit cards
No reservations taken

遠東樓

South China Cafe

That it should feed two people for less than $10 seems a reasonable thing to ask of a reasonable restaurant. If we told you that five (count them, from your pinky to your thumb—five) people could dine for that price—well, you'd probably think we were having nightmares from our bratwurst.

We can't explain how, but the South China Cafe does it. And its combination dinners include five or six dishes, plus fortune cookies and tea. If you don't want to go the combination route, pick some of the superb *a la carte* dishes. We particularly enjoyed beef with oyster sauce and ginger beef, but none of the selections was disappointing.

This restaurant is a barren little place with a few ceiling-high booths, a long counter and some tables in back. But if you're hungry, not too rich, and in the mood for good basic Chinese food, even your mother couldn't feed you better for less.

4133 18th St., San Francisco; (415) 861-9323
Mon., Tues., Thurs., Sat., Sun. 11:30 - 10:00;
  Fri. 11:30 - 11:00; closed Wed.
No bar
No credit cards
Reservations essential for 4 or more

Sun Hung Heung

Walking through Chinatown can be an incredibly distracting experience. The sights and smells alone could dizzy you and leave you lost. Our favorite haven at times like these is Sun Hung Hueng, a large, comparatively posh restaurant with excellent food.

When you enter, ask to be seated upstairs, where there is more privacy and less noise. Then settle into the menu, and we recommend that you order *a la carte*. There are many exciting and tempting choices, but don't hesitate to order unfamiliar dishes. You will not be unpleasantly surprised. Each dish at Sun Hung Hueng is carefully prepared and served individually to allow you to savor the intriguing flavors. Some of our favorite selections include chicke with plum sauce, beef yee mein, pork with snow peas, and shrimp with cashews. If you are particularly fond of cashews, this last dish will amaze you, for there appear to be three or four whole cashew nuts for every shrimp, and there are plenty of shrimp. This kind of attention to quality and lack of compromise is evident in all the dishes at Sun Hung Hueng.

We do recommend that you make reservations, however, for many people have discovered that this is one of the few places left where quality remains paramount. Even if you have to wait to be seated, be assured that here you won't be hustled off into the bar—unless, of course, you volunteer.

744 Washington St., San Francisco; (415) 982-2319
Mon., Wed. - Fri. 11:30 - 1:00 a.m.; Sat. & Sun.
 11:30 - 3:00 a.m.; closed Tues.
Full bar
BA, MC
Reservations advisable

Sun Ya

Sun Ya looks as though it had started out trying to be a tourist-catcher, then squandered most of its capital on the large outside canopy and blinking lights. The decoration budget stretched only far enough to build a small rock garden halfway down the stairs. Not that the interior of Sun Ya isn't finished—it just seems incongruously plain compared to the pretentious facade. The restaurant is immaculate and neat, with some Oriental art placed casually around the room. Even more art, however, is evident in the preparation of the food.

Ordering from the *a la carte* menu (combination dinners are also available) will really test your will power. The reasonable prices will make it even harder to limit yourself. If you'd like some direction, we particularly enjoyed the abalone soup, curry prawns, combination bean cake, chicken with Chinese mushrooms and crabmeat chop suey. There are lots of exciting possibilities, so bring your friends and really chow down (no relation to chow mein).

823 Clay St., San Francisco; (415) 982-0922
Daily 11:30 - 10:15
Beer & wine
BA, MC
Reservations advisable

Ya Su Yuan

Ya Su Yuan looks just like the neighborhood
Chinese restaurant you'd find anywhere. It is
located on the outskirts of Chinatown, and its
ordinary facade has probably saved it from an on-
slaught of tourists and a concurrent price hike.
Because, surely, if more people were aware of the
taste treats awaiting them here, it would become
as popular as many of its more glamorous relatives
down the block and around the corner.

This is one of the places where local Chinese
dine on Mandarin-style food—a far cry from the
Cantonese fare that usually abounds. Most fun
is to run down the *a la carte* menu and try some
of the excellent Mandarin dishes. For example, a
good selection might include mu shi pork (a combination of pork, egg, onions, carrots and other
vegetables) plus a side order of "pancakes" in which
to roll the mu shi pork; Mandarin beef; and a unique
vegetable dish such as Chinese cabbage with white
sauce. Or you can get a family dinner that includes
a fair, but not exciting, selection of dishes.

This is definitely not a fancy place, but a terrific
place to try Mandarin delicacies. If you're really
brave, you could even put together a combination
of cold jellyfish, pork and preserved turnip soup,
sauteed pork kidney and braised sea cucumber. If
you didn't know what you were eating, it might be
even more delicious.

638 Pacific Ave., San Francisco; (415) 986-7386
Tues. - Sun. 11:00 - 10:00; closed Mon.
Beer & wine
BA, MC
Reservations advisable

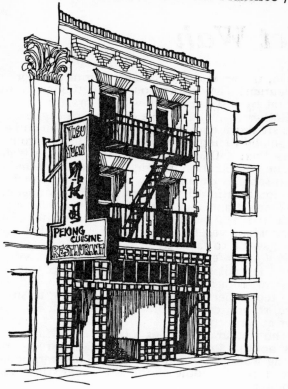

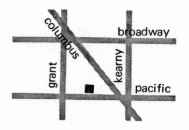

Yet Wah

Oh, the aromas that emanate from this corner restaurant! They make you feel as though you could get fat by just taking a few deep breaths.

Rather than taking this chance, we suggest that you sit down and really enjoy putting on some weight by dining on a selection of dishes from the more than 250 Mandarin items on the Yet Wah menu.

The combination dinners here include some pretty good samples of this spicy cuisine. Surprisingly, even the combination dinner for two offers Mongolian beef, sweet-and-sour pork and cashew chicken, along with an appetizer and rice. This is definitely not a place where vegetables are so dominant that everything seems to taste green.

If you prefer to go the *a la carte* route, you might try pot stickers, sizzling rice soup, one of the unusual lamb dishes and a seafood or fowl dish. The recommended list is much too long to supply here, so you can feel pretty safe just picking whatever appeals to you.

The restaurant itself is a one-room affair with a few booths, some Chinese lanterns and red curtains at the windows. Food this good, however, could be served in the middle of the street and still taste delicious.

1801 and 1829 Clement St., San Francisco;
(415) 387-8040, (415) 387-8056
Daily 4:00 - 11:00
Beer & wine
All major credit cards
No reservations taken

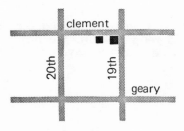

Claus & Gigi's

One day we spotted a parked car that had a sign on it advertising "Claus & Gigi's Kitchen." We wrote down the address, visited the place and immediately fell in love. Would you believe home delivery of fillet of sole meuniere, prawns provencale or paprika veal? Or if you don't want to pamper yourself by having Claus and Gigi deliver the dishes to your home, you can dine in their miniscule restaurant (three tables seating a total of about twelve comfortably) and watch Claus prepare and serve these delicacies.

Once you've gotten over the initial shock that a restaurant like this really does exist—eat! Everything is beautifully prepared, and if you don't feel like a complete dinner (with fresh vegetables, potatoes or rice and a green salad), there are also hot and cold sandwiches and soup. The sandwiches are spectacular; Polish sausage and sauerkraut on a French roll, served with German potato salad, is particularly good. Claus also makes one of the finest samples of chocolate mousse we've tried.

If you need more encouragement, you must not be hungry.

1525 Irving St., San Francisco; (415) 681-9111
Mon. - Sat. 12:00 - 2:00, 5:00 - 10:30; closed Sun.
No bar
No credit cards
Reservations advisable

Note: Claus & Gigi's has closed temporarily but hopes to reopen soon. We hope so too because we really enjoyed the food.

Europa

The Europa restaurant is an ivy-covered retreat into the world of continental cooking. The owners, Jerry and Anna Prill, run the whole show and see to your comfort.

They call their restaurant a Wiener schnitzel house, but the scope of the menu is wide. In fact, when we asked Jerry to recommend something, he suggested the veal paprikash and the special ham, baked earlier that day. Both entrees came with several slices of Hungarian bohemian dumplings, plus red cabbage. There was more than enough good food. Other entrees include Wiener schnitzel, smoked lean pork, sauerbraten, roast beef, goulash, beef bourgignon and bratwurst.

While you're dining on this delicious fare, you can sneak a peek at the cooking talents being displayed in the kitchen in the center of the restaurant. Or you can admire Anna in her flowered skirt and embroidered apron. You might even chat with the locals who seem to frequent the restaurant regularly.

Our only disappointment was the apple strudel, which we were told was not homemade, but from a local bakery. It simply was not of equal quality with the rest of the food.

2769 Lombard St., San Francisco; (415) 567-0361
Mon. - Sat. 4:00 - 11:30; Sun. 6:00 - 11:00
Beer & wine
MC
No reservations taken

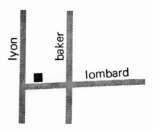

Recovery Room

Aptly named because of its proximity to a major medical center, the Recovery Room is also a haven for those of us not medicinally inclined. Unfortunately, not many people at a time can recover here, because there are only about eight or ten tables. The size gives the restaurant a feeling of intimacy, and the tasteful decor adds to this atmosphere.

Everything here is continental. Fresh flowers adorn the black tablecloths, water is served only if requested and the wine list is actually a book-sized catalog. The menu runs the gamut from escargots to bratwurst to veal piccata to chicken Bombay. Whether the dish is French, Italian or German, it is bound to be delectable. Both the soup and the salad are excellent, and the house dressing is exceptionally good. Portions of everything are abundant.

All entrees are around $5 or less; so unless you really splurge on something from the fantastic wine list, the only condition you'll need to recover from is a full stomach.

94 Judah St., San Francisco; (415) 681-4010
Lunch: Wed. - Fri. 11:30 - 2:00; Dinner: Tues. -
  Sat. 5:30 - 9:00; closed Sun. & Mon.
Beer & wine
No credit cards
Reservations advisable

Coffee Renaissance

Ideally, crepes should be served by quaintly braided waitresses in cute little restaurants with checkered curtains. Ideally, crepes shouldn't cost an arm and a leg. Unfortunately, the two ideals don't seem to go together. However, if you can put up with ordering your crepes at a counter, picking them up when your number is called and eating them at unfancy tables in a restaurant where the decorations are empty coffee-bean sacks, you may end up with a pleasantly full stomach and all your limbs intact. You can test this theory by eating at the Coffee Renaissance.

You may not even know where you're eating, since the sign outside says simply Espresso—Crepes. But here, all crepes are in the $2 range, and you can even get a crepe with apricot jam plus a cup of cappuccino for about a dollar. The crepes come either stuffed with such typical goodies as ham, cheese and spinach, or as dessert crepes topped with fresh fruit and your choice of whipped or sour cream.

This is a particularly fun place if you sit by the front window and watch the Berkeley parade. If you're not hungry, take advantage of the view and enjoy one of the many varieties of coffee available here

2512 Durant Ave., Berkeley; (415) 548-6977
Mon. - Fri. 9:00 a.m. - midnight; Sat. 10:00 a.m. -
  midnight; Sun. 10:00 a.m. - 11:00 p.m.
No bar
No credit cards
No reservations taken

Cuba

If you think an empty restaurant means there's something wrong inside, you'll miss many opportunities for exciting dining experiences. If we had operated on that premise, we never would have discovered the Cuba restaurant, which was surprisingly empty when we visited.

The large dining room is neat and gaily decorated with plastic ferns and palms, white tablecloths and re place mats and chairs. Much more intriguing is the menu: reading it is like exploring an undiscovered gastronomic universe. The seafood here is exceptional. We tried the camarones enchilados—shrimp Cuban style, served in a light tomato sauce with onions, peas and a slice of yucca. (Yucca, by the way, is similar in consistency to potato—but not quite the same.) We also tried the roast pork, which was (as the menu stated) tender and delicious, and very generously sliced.

Most dinners include French bread and butter, salad, rice, black beans and yucca or fries. Be brave and try the yucca. You won't find it anywhere else.

2886 16th St., San Francisco; (415) 626-9871
Fri. - Wed. 12:00 - 10:00; closed Thurs.
Beer & wine
No credit cards
Reservations advisable

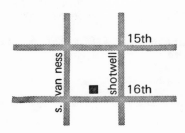

Melting Pot

Fondue restaurants are definitely a lot of fun and definitely not places for gourmet dining. The Melting Pot is a good choice for this particular kind of experience because it offers really good fondues, any one of which can be filling enough to serve as a meal.

There isn't a fondue here that isn't smooth and clingy. The variations include shrimp, ham, salami, beef or mushrooms in a cheese base, and each one is packed with chunky additions. (Of course, there is the plain cheese version, also.) The servings of both the fondue dip and the bread cubes are very generous.

An exceptionally good bittersweet chocolate fondue is available here. Served with squares of cream cheese, marshmallows, mandarin orange slices, maraschino cherries and pieces of fresh apple and pineapple, it is guaranteed to satisfy your sweet tooth for a long time.

The Melting Pot is roughly put together; there are even some exposed light bulbs on the ceiling. But there are also oil paintings on the walls and there is entertainment on Friday and Saturday nights, so I guess it's just a matter of where you put your priorities.

2505 Hearst Ave., Berkeley; (415) 843-4354.
  Brown Ave. at Mt. Diablo, La Fayette;
  (415) 283-1730. N. Main St., Walnut Creek;
  (415) 937-1006
Sun. - Thurs. 5 - 10; Fri. & Sat. 5 - 11
Beer & wine
No credit cards
Reservations advisable

Le Chateau

The next time you're in the neighborhood of Chinatown, but simply can't look a pea pod in the eye, think Le Chateau.

Across the street from the ornate Chinatown entrance, this cafe seems completely unaffected by the massive Oriental influence practically next door. Its arched windows let in buckets of sunlight as you sit at marble-topped wrought-iron tables choosing from such continental dishes as Vienna schnitzel, meatballs, liver, filet of sole, omelettes and ham— not even a token egg roll. Dinners include soup or salad, vegetables, potatoes or rice and ice cream or sherbet. Prices range from $3 to $5 for a complete dinner.

A lot of attention to detail is evident here. For example, the dinner salad includes fresh peas and carrots. While the restaurant is immaculate, a warm feeling is created by the green and gold color scheme, the high ceilings and the soft music.

The Paris cafe atmosphere seems to attract many people who simply walk in instead of walking by. So if you enjoy people-watching along with your supper, you'll find plenty of diversion at Le Chateau And the cheesecake is marvelous.

323 Grant Ave., San Francisco; (415) 781-6730
Sun. - Fri. 8 - 8; Sat. 8 - 5
Beer & wine
BA, MC
Reservations advisable

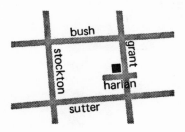

Tricolor

A reasonably priced, authentic French restaurant? They disappeared with Humphrey Bogart - Ingrid Bergman movies, right? *Mais non.*

Waving the colors of the French flag, the Tricolor restaurant makes fine French cuisine available to those of us who don't like the feeling that air fare has been added to the dinner bill.

But aside from the attractive prices, this is a special restaurant in other ways. The atmosphere is pleasant and gay, the service extremely efficient and the food *extraordinaire.* With such enticing entrees as chicken saute chasseur, pot roast Bretonne, boeuf bourgignon, tripes a la mode de Caen, coq au vin, veal Cordon Bleu and breast of capon a la Kiev, decisions are difficult. And once you're decided, it's not just a commitment to the entree; for the price of dinner also includes hors d'oeuvres, soup du jour, Tricolor salad, vegetables, potatoes du jour, dessert and tea or coffee.

This is quite a different approach from that of French restaurants where everything is *a la carte* and priced as high as the Eiffel Tower. *Vive le difference.*

4233 Geary Blvd., San Francisco; (415) 752-9974
Wed. - Sat. 5 - 10; Sun. 3 - 9; closed Mon. & Tues.
Beer & wine
No credit cards
No reservations taken

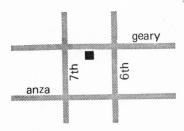

German Cook

It's hard to top this place for excellent home-cooked German dinners served in a quaint European environment. The seating is limited to only three booths and seven counter stools, but generally a wait of 15 minutes is all that is required. That will provide ample time to survey the conglomeration of articles hanging on the walls and suspended from the ceiling. The wooden booths are painted in a Scandanavian pattern of tulips drifting on a white background.

As you listen to the soft stereo sounds of the old country, try the stuffed pork chops, veal cutlet or Polish sausage. Each dinner is served with fried potatoes and cabbage that even people who claim to dislike cabbage will not be able to resist. The food is served piping hot from the stove by a smiling waitress with a snappy German accent. A special is also posted each day in the front window. If a rich dessert is your thing with after-dinner coffee, sample the German chocolate cake. For drink you can choose German wine and beer as well as domestic beer. If you are in a hurry or by yourself, sit at the counter, visit with the owner/chef and watch the food being prepared.

612 O'Farrel St., San Francisco; (415) 776-9022
Mon. - Sat. 4:30 - 9:30; closed Sun.
Beer & wine
No credit cards
Reservations advisable

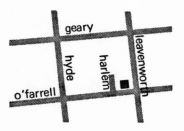

Hans H. Speckmann

German food is the specialty of Hans H. Speckmann, Inc., II, and it is offered in every imaginable form. For dining, the restaurant is available. For dining and concentrated drinking, try the Bierstube. If you want to create masterpieces at home, you can even order from the delicatessen.

But why not take the easy way out and let the restaurant do the work that it does so well? Your only challenge will be to pronounce the dishes you want. How about rouladen mit salzkartoffeln und rotkohl (stuffed beef rolls and red cabbage)? Or maybe gekockter schinken mit Schweizer kaese (buffet ham with Swiss cheese) is more to your taste.

Dinners are served with new potatoes and other varied vegetables. Only the goulash, stuffed beef rolls and fried smoked pork entrees are served regularly along with daily specials. Sausage plates and open-face sandwiches are also on the menu.

Service can sometimes be slow, but the food is good and plentiful. This is a neighborhood restaurant—so if you're in the neighborhood, try it. In fact, it's worth going out of your way for.

1550 Church St., San Francisco; (415) 282-6850
Mon. - Thurs. 10 - 7; Fri. 10 - 8; Sat. 10 - 7;
*   Sun. 12 - 6*
Beer & wine
No credit cards
No reservations taken

Budapest West

Class? There seems to be some debate on its definition. At Budapest West, class doesn't mean expensive. It means good taste—in both the food and the decor. It also means a romantic setting, with fresh flowers on the table and waiters in formal attire. Most of all, it means fine Hungarian food, prepared as it is nowhere else in San Francisco.

Dinners include Hungarian classics such as goulash, chicken paprika and stuffed cabbage. The versatility of the Hungarian palate is truly evident in the combinations of ingredients, which sound cacophonous to the Western palate but taste harmonious. The best example of this is the Transylvanian goulash (yes, Boris, there really is a Transylvania), which is a pork goulash cooked in sauerkraut with sour cream, served with layered potatoes. Delicious!

After dinner, try a dobos torte or one of the assorted pastries. You may think you won't have room, but their mere appearance is so delectable that they're impossible to resist.

3011 Steiner St., San Francisco; (415) 921-2141
Tues. - Sat. 5:30 - 10:15; Sun. 4:30 - 10:15;
   closed Mon.
Beer & wine
BA, MC
No reservations taken

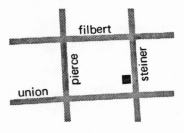

Bit of Indonesia

Other than Amsterdam, there probably isn't a place better than Bit of Indonesia to get an introduction to Indonesian food.

This is definitely a feasting place. When you're here, your mind should be on nothing but food. The surroundings provide no distractions from the marvelous fare, except for the sometimes too-evident lack of air conditioning.

As you sit at one of the small, crowded tables covered by batik tablecloths, try to concentrate on the different flavors and textures which comprise the Indonesian menu. If you've never tried it before, order the rystaffel, which includes a little bit of everything. For the best selection, go with a party of four or five people, let everyone taste all the dishes in the rystaffel, and then order individual entrees.

The food here is seasoned perfectly and the sauces, especially on the meat dishes, are exceptional. A sample of the particularly outstanding dishes might include egg roll with peanut sauce, spiced barbecued chicken, marinated beef on a skewer, beef in Javanese curry, vegetables with peanut sauce and chicken with spices.

211 Clement St., San Francisco; (415) 752-4042
Tues. - Sun. 5 - 10; closed Mon.
Beer only
No credit cards
No reservations taken

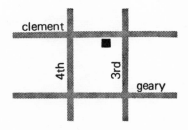

Indonesian Village

At the Indonesian Village, the menu strays just slightly from the traditional dishes of the rystaffel—and onto some new and exciting paths for even the experienced Indonesian diner.

The rystaffel for two is around $12—so, in order to stay in our price range and yet try a variety of dishes, we suggest that you bring three other people. All of you can then sample the rystaffel and order whatever else appeals to you. The rystaffel includes shrimp chips (with a consistency similar to potato chips, but lighter and not greasy), a light broth with vegetables and noodles, vegetable salad with peanut sauce, vegetable egg rolls, potato balls, a skewer of broiled chicken or pork, chicken in a special sauce, squash and carrots, two kinds of rice with shredded coconut, lime sherbet and tea or coffee. *A la carte* dinners are also available, all quite reasonably priced.

The restaurant is not well known yet, so it is quiet and relaxed and the service is very personal. Hopefully, the service will stay the same even if we spread the word a little. It seems a shame for a restaurant of this quality to go virtually unnoticed.

2006 9th St., Berkeley; (415) 841-9667
Wed. - Mon. 5:30 - 10; closed Tues.
Beer & wine
No credit cards
Reservations advisable

Moestopo's

Moestopo's is an Indonesian restaurant that emphasizes individual dishes rather than the rystaffel.

This is a small place, run by a family that obviously takes pride in its cooking. While it offers many dishes found at most Indonesian restaurants, the choice of 15 entrees here also includes rainbow trout, tahu tjampur (fried bean cakes mixed with bean sprouts, peanuts, shrimp chips and rice, topped with a special sauce), and mie goreng (pan-fried noodles topped with shredded cabbage, Chinese greens, onion greens, celery, fried crisp onion flakes and chicken). There are also two special desserts: spekkoek (cinnamon cake) and srikaja (coconut pudding). Several of the dishes are served with a well-seasoned and delicious curry sauce. A combination plate—a somewhat unusual offering for an Indonesian restaurant—is also available.

The decor is rather nondescript, with candles on the tables and Indonesian items decorating the walls. But the food is outstanding and its taste will stick in your mind as well as in your stomach.

Entree prices start at about $1.50 and go to about $3.50. The rystaffel is slightly more than $10 for two.

4036 Balboa St., San Francisco; (415) 752-5809
Wed. - Sat. 4 - 10; closed Mon. & Tues.
Beer & wine
MC
Reservations advisable

MOESTOPO'S

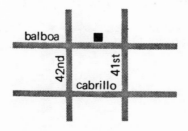

Caffe Giovanni

Mama Savaria's homemade minestrone soup is so good that a bowl (or two, if you're really hungry) with bread and a glass of wine would be a perfect dinner at Caffe Giovanni. The soup is almost stew-thick and joyfully packed with meat and fresh vegetables. However, if you're more interested in great pasta, such as delicious baked lasagne, cannelloni or spaghetti with tender meatballs, you'll find these here, too. The pizza is also quite good. Whatever you pick, it's going to be well prepared and filling.

The *"Caffe"* part of the restaurant's name comes from the sidewalk cafe at the very front where, weather permitting, you can dine *al fresco*. There are two other dining areas: the cavernous, dimly lit main dining room and the Boat House, a smaller dining area decorated with hatch covers and stuffed sailfish.

Caffe Giovanni can be an intimate setting for two or a congenial setting for many more. You can sit at booths or tables, and the service is good enough to handle large parties easily. If you're feeling really good and want to maintain your mood, you might try something from "Il Bar." How about a banana cow: a rum, lime juice and banana concoction. *Squisito!*

2420 Shattuck Ave., Berkeley; (415) 843-6678
Sun. - Thurs. 11 - 1; Fri. & Sat. 11 - 2 a.m.
Full bar
No credit cards
No reservations taken

Eduardo's

If you're looking for a small, intimate, family-run Italian restaurant that exudes warmth and delicious aromas, Eduardo's is your light at the end of the tunnel.

And Eduardo himself has a lot to do with casting that glow. He's always there—acting as host, waiter or bill collector—and his friendly accent adds to the evenings' enjoyment. In fact, you get a welcome feeling that minute you walk into this charming restaurant.

The cooking is done in the dining room; the two areas are separated by a low brick wall adorned with plants. Another wall is literally jammed with pictures that provide many moments of interesting diversion.

The star attraction here—sharing the spotlight with Eduardo, of course—is the food. Pasta specialties such as green lasagne, fettucini carbonara and cannelloni Eduard's are so light and delicious that you can make them disappear from your platter practically by inhaling. Lamb, beef, pork and chicken entrees are also available, but we definitely recommend the pasta above all.

2234 Chestnut St., San Francisco; (415) 567-6164
Tues. - Sun. 5 - 10:30; closed Mon.
Beer & wine
No credit cards
No reservations taken

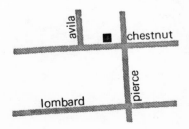

Granata's

You want a steak, your girlfriend wants "something different" and your friends just want to go someplace off the beaten path. Aha! Granata's.

This place is so far off the beaten path that the employees probably send messages to the outside world via homing pigeon. And after you taste the food, you'll know why the pigeons would always come home.

Once you've blazed the trail, try the baked manicotti for the "something different." This is an Italian delicacy of fresh ricotta cheese seasoned with fine herbs, lightly rolled in egg batter and topped with Italian sauce. It is so light and delicious that it will probably be the item you return for.

If this doesn't make your tower lean, try one of the special dinners. For $1 more than the *a la carte* entrees, you also get soup, salad, pasta, coffee and dessert. The dinners include filet kabob, veal and various chicken dishes, and all but a couple are in our price range.

2730 9th St. at Pardee, Berkeley; (415) 845-9571
Sun. - Fri. 11:30 a.m. - midnight; Fri. & Sat.
  11:30 a.m. - 2 a.m.
Full bar
AE, BA, MC
Reservations advisable

BERKELEY
pardee
9th
grayson
10th

Iron Pot

In the heart of the sedate financial district is the noisy, friendly Iron Pot Italian restaurant. Here you can cry in your beer over a declining stock or boisterously brag about a big deal. And there are so many people talking at the same time that you won't have to worry about giving away any secrets.

Instead, you can worry about how you're going to eat all the food put in front of you. Because each dinner comes with appetizers, soup, salad, entree and pasta. And most of the menu is under $4.

The appetizers include slices of salami and prosciutto, and the soup is served in a tureen that is left on your table in case you want seconds. For your main course, you can choose from chicken, veal, pasta, roast beef, ham, fish, steak or chops. You can accompany your meal with a glass of California wine, and if you're a sports fan you can probably catch your favorite game on the TV in the bar. Or, if you're more aesthetically inclined, you can enjoy the works of local artists which decorate the walls.

639 Montgomery St., San Francisco; (415) 392-2100
Mon. - Sat. 4 - 10; closed Sun.
Full bar
BA
Reservations advisable

La Ginestra

Mill Valley is inspiringly beautiful, almost unrealistically so. One good way to remind yourself that real people live here is to eat at La Ginestra

This is real food: delicious, generous portions served with a little extra love. While more waiters would speed up the service, it would be hard to match the one that is already here. He is extremely helpful in explaining the various dishes (and this Italian menu contains some unusual items) and will tell you specifically why he recommends one dish over another. He must have a hard time deciding, because everything here is so good. We thought the veal dishes particularly well prepared, although the pasta was also outstanding. The salads are big and fresh, and the desserts, especially the spumoni and zabaglione, are excellent. House wines are Valley of the Moon and very nice.

The interior is uninspired, with unclothed tables, a fish net across the ceiling, and no air conditioning. But it's a very comfortable spot, and in this setting, even the finest decor couldn't compete with the beauty outside your window.

127 Throckmorton Ave., Mill Valley; (415) 388-0224
Tues. - Sun. 12 - 2, 5 - 11; closed Mon.
Beer & wine
No credit cards
Reservations advisable

MILL VALLEY

Old Spaghetti Factory

If you're observant and hungry, the Old Spaghetti Factory will be a feast for both your eyes and your stomach. It perches about one-third of the way up one of those incredible San Francisco hills and looks as if all the bright colors and funny objects in the city had slid down the hill and collided right there.

As you walk past the gaily painted picket fence that leads you to the restaurant entrance, you're positive that you're going to get lost between the buildings. But where the fence ends, the fun begins. You enter a room bedecked with chairs hanging from the ceiling, cotton-puff clouds suspended on strings, white Roman pillars placed every which way, clotheslines, ivy, and every imaginable form of furniture to sit on. If one of the latter is vacant, grab it quickly, for a major part of the restaurant's decorative charm is the people—lots of them. And the lines can get long.

Obviously, all those people are not waiting just to stare at the cracks in the wooden tables. For here you get a feast-size pile of spaghetti topped with your choice of sauces, plus garlic bread and a green salad, all for about $3. While the salad is unspectacular, the spaghetti is delicious. And seconds are free! We were particularly fond of the meat sauce, and a little disappointed with the mushroom sauce. In addition, there is a super lasagne, chunky with cheese and sausage. And the garlic bread basket is kept full without your needing to ask.

478 Green St., San Francisco; (415) 421-0221
Daily 5:30 - 11
Beer & wine
No credit cards
Reservations not taken

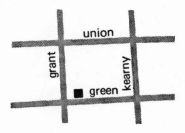

O Sole Mio

Strolling guitarists are fairly common, but singing waiters who compete with the recorded voices of Mario Lanza, Ezio Pinza and Enrico Caruso are not only rare, they're brave. At O Sole Mio, this entertainment is part of the charm.

From its new, modern facade, you would never guess that the interior of O Sole Mio is warm and reminiscent of old Italy. However, once you are inside, the murals on the wall and the bunches of fruit clinging to overhead trellises provide a delightful setting for anything from lasagne to pizza.

While many varieties of pasta are available and the pizza is highly recommended, the lasagne here should be sampled. The veal parmigiana and chicken cacciatore are also excellent. In fact, O Sole Mio seems completely in tune with some of the best Italian food available in the city.

2031 Chestnut St., San Francisco; (415) 931-9008
Sun. - Thurs. 11 - 2, 4 - midnight; Fri. & Sat.
*   11 - 2, 4 - 1:30 a.m.*
Beer & wine
MC
Reservations not taken

San Remo

The dining rooms of the San Remo hotel look like a setting for a *Twilight Zone* episode about the 1940s. They are huge and look eerie when they're devoid of customers. Except for the few booths (some with curtains), dining is done at long family-style tables. The selections on the jukebox in the adjoining bar range from Guy Lombardo to Paul McCartney.

While the seating is family style, the huge portions of food are served individually. On our last visit, most dinners were between $3.50 and $4. If you order a complete dinner, you get a green salad, soup du jour, ravioli or spaghetti, ice cream and coffee in addition to your entree. Every course is tasty and prepared with a little extra care. For example, the salad has carrots, beets and beans as well as lettuce, and the french fries are crisp and definitely not greasy.

We tried the chicken livers en brochette with bacon and they were fresh and tender, while the breaded veal cutlets were served with an imaginative gravy. Other entrees include ham, pasta, pork chops, veal, chicken and incredible sweetbreads sauteed with mushroom sauce.

Dress casually, bring the kids (if you have any and you feed them) and really enjoy some good cooking.

2237 Mason St., San Francisco; (415) 673-9090
Wed. - Sat. 4 - 9:45; Sun. noon - 9:45; closed
*   Mon. & Tues.*
Full bar
No credit cards
Reservations advisable

The Sausage Factory

There are few restaurants where you can take notes, give somebody the notes to read, and be assured that they will get the feeling of the place. At the Sausage Factory, however, your first impressions are apt to be the most vivid and the most honest. For that reason, we have strayed from our usual routine and hereby quote directly from our scribbled notes:

"Busy, so wait in the back room. The walk back to the waiting room seems almost dangerous—no doors are labeled and you're never sure where you'll end up when you push them open. The place looks like they've cleaned out everybody's mothers' garages and stored the stuff in this waiting room. Full of old couches and chairs, so comfortable that you're tempted to fall asleep. Atmosphere in this room is kind of hippie - ski lodge. Everybody sits around and talks and drinks. Even the dining room looks like they had a decoration party—everybody just ran up to the walls and attached his favorite stuff somehow."

While this is not the most articulate description, it does convey the casual, cluttered atmosphere of the Sausage Factory. We were very happy with its pizza but disappointed in the lasagne, which tasted like a pizza casserole. Other entrees include ravioli, eggplant parmigiana, cannelloni, veal, sausage, spaghetti and chicken. Dinners come with chunky minestrone soup or crisp salad, bread with lots of soft butter, and coffee. And the house wine is very nice.

517 Castro St., San Francisco; (415) 626-4252
Daily 11 a.m. - midnight
Beer & wine
No credit cards
No reservations taken

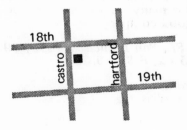

622-Ristorante Italiano

Don't sit down at the 622 Ristorante Italiano unless you plan on staying, because you will be served the first course of dinner before you are told what the entrees are for that evening. So if you don't want to take pot luck (and we've never been unlucky here), ask what's for dinner before you're settled in.

Once you decide that you're in the mood for a food extravaganza, prepare yourself to consume soup, salad, pasta, your choice from three entrees (we were offered stuffed veal, roast beef or roast chicken), vegetables and dessert (usually fruit and cheese). Soup can be practically anything—we enjoyed the noodle soup—and is definitely home-made. Salad, with a good house dressing, includes beets as well as lettuce and tomatoes. Our pasta was spaghetti with an excellent meat sauce.

This is a friendly place that seems to stimulate loud, enthusiastic conversations. Everyone is convivial, so don't be surprised if the strangers seated at your table assume that you would like to chat. Decor is simple, with green and white checked oilcloths covering the tables, wooden chairs and tile floors. There are only nine tables, and the focal point of the restaurant seems to be the long bar. It's the kind of place that reminds you that, for many, dinner is a time to enjoy good food and good company.

622 Green St., San Francisco; (415) 392-3645
Daily 11:45 - 2, 5:30 - 9:30
Full bar
No credit cards
Reservations advisable

Sorrento

A lot of restaurants that try to be romantic by dimming their lights give you the impression that either they're trying to cut back on their electric bill or they don't want you to see the spots on the glasses. On the other hand, some restaurants can create a mood easily because the atmosphere is total and every aspect of the decor is attuned to the mood.

At Sorrento, you experience such a mood. The waiters are charming, the decor is tastefully done and the food is excellent. Even the wait to be seated is made more palatable if you sit on the outdoor wooden bench with an arched wooden canopy which is provided just for that purpose.

For dinner, you can choose from such entrees as pasta, eggplant, veal, chicken or seafood. Dinner includes soup or a large salad and fresh vegetables, prepared and seasoned beautifully. All portions are very large and nicely presented, and the food is so good that you'll probably force yourself to eat it all or take it home.

Other than the effort you'll make to clean your plate, you'll have an effortless and relaxing evening. When we were there, the staff even gave each woman a carnation after the meal.

2141 Polk St., San Francisco; (415) 474-0422
Daily 5 - midnight
Beer & wine
BA, MC
Reservations advisable

Vagabond Villa

The Vagabond Villa near Pedro Point is rumored to have been a storehouse for bootleggers during Prohibition. At least that's what the restaurant's menu claims.

The menu also describes dinners so voluminous that it's nearly impossible to finish all the good food set before you. Because with the complete dinner you get an appetizer plate with olives, green onions, pepperoncini, ceci vinaigrette, celery and pickled pigs' knuckles (when available). Then soup, salad, spaghetti, potatoes and vegetables. Enough? Well, what about your entree? There's veal scaloppini or parmigiana, fillet of sole, scallops, prawns, oysters or ground sirloin—all around $5 or $6. Broiler selections, priced higher, are also available.

Obviously, with quantity and prices like this, not a great deal is spent on overhead. However, the Vagabond Villa is a very comfortable place, with a fireplace in front and Christmas tree lights lit all year 'round. And with all that good food, you'll really feel welcome.

404 San Pedro Rd., Pacifica; (415) 359-2552
Daily 5 - 10:30
Full bar
MC
Reservations advisable

Victor's Pizza

Some of us have always wanted to be circus aerialists or treasure-hunting scuba divers. But for food freaks, the supreme accomplishment would be to become an expert pizza twirler. If this is the kind of talent you respect, you can watch the ceremonies at Victor's Pizza and then ingest the resulting masterpiece.

The pizza is made in full view of the public. You can watch through the window or stand at the counter and gaze. Ingredients are picked from huge bowls full of cheese, mushrooms and meats and tossed on a seemingly innocuous dough, which then rises to a thick and crusty goodness that envelops all the terrific things on its surface.

If you don't want to try the pizza (what foolishness!), you can dine in the back room on veal scalloppini, eggplant or Italian sausage, all of quality outstanding enough to make your decision difficult.

1411 Polk St., San Francisco; (415) 885-1660
Wed. - Mon. 11 - 11:30; closed Tues.
Beer & wine
No credit cards
No reservations taken

Hisamatsu

I sometimes think that part of the reason Japanese dinners taste so good is that they usually look so good.

At Hisamatsu, the presentation of the food adds immensely to its appeal. You can enjoy your meal sitting country-style at low tables or American-style in booths. The waitresses are all dressed authentically and somehow manage to serve you efficiently while taking those little dainty steps.

This is not an elegant restaurant, but it is very comfortable. The menu includes a variety of *a la carte* dishes in addition to some interesting combination dinners that may be ordered by one person, rather than the usual minimum of two. These combination dinners are not inexpensive, but they are a wise investment.

Our favorite combination is the Ume dinner, which includes clear broth, fresh vegetable salad with Japanese vinegar dressing, shrimp tempura, beef teriyaki, condiments, rice and dessert. The tempura includes vegetables and two large butterfly shrimp, and the serving of beef is tender and generous.

1655 Market St., San Francisco; (415) 626-3828
Lunch: 11:30 - 2; Dinner: Mon. - Thurs. 5 - 10;
   Fri. & Sat. 5 - 11; closed Sun.
Beer & wine
No credit cards
Reservations advisable

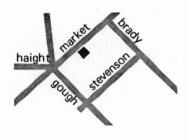

Korean Inn

When you arrive at the Korean Inn, be sure to ask for a table upstairs so you can enjoy the mood created by sitting at a low table on a big, soft pillow. (If you prefer conventional seating, you can dine at one of the small tables downstairs.) And don't be afraid to order the combination dinner. The component dishes are truly representative and superlative.

With these things in mind, you can expect a really enjoyable dining experience. The cook, Mrs. Jung Yun Chai, has written a book on Oriental cooking, and she prepares tempting treats that will surprise your palate. Bul-kogi, consisting of thin slices of marinated beef, is especially delicious. Sinsul-lo is a cross between a soup and a stew with meat, fresh mushrooms, water chestnuts, bean curd and other good things. (The menu claims that the latter was President Eisenhower's favorite dish when he visited Korea.) The extraordinary salad, which consists of a spicy mixture of Oriental vegetables, is unusually flavorful. In addition to these dishes, the combination dinner also includes Korean spareribs, fried shrimp (similar to tempura), barbecued chicken, rice, tea and a special dessert of mandarin orange slices and pineapple.

The service is excellent and dishes are generally served one at a time—a symbol of the care and attention both the food and the patrons receive at the Korean Inn.

1329 Gilman St., Berkeley; (415) 524-7732
Tues. - Sun. 5 - 9; closed Mon.
Beer & wine
MC
Reservations advisable

BERKELEY

El Charro

How we love tostadas! Especially the kind that is piled so high that it's an expedition to get to the bottom, and you're never quite sure what you're going to find along the way. At El Charro, you will find either beef or chicken, beans, at least a whole avocado, cheese, peas, corn, string beans and tomatoes.

You can also find less flamboyant but equally tasty dishes. One fine example of the cooking skill here is the dish called flautas. Similar to what most people know as taquitas, these are deep-fried, stuffed with string beef and topped with sour cream. Dinners include beans, rice, salad and tortillas; they range from combination plates to chorizo con huevo (sausage with eggs). And if you've ever wanted to know the difference between burritos and enchiladas, the menu at El Charro explains it to you. Both Mexican and domestic beers are available for washing down the flavorful food.

205 Grand Ave., South San Francisco; (415)
873-1993
Tues. - Sat. 11 - 10; Sun. 11 - 8; closed Mon.
Beer & wine
No credit cards
Reservations advisable

El Toreador Fonda Mejicana

The food here looks so delicious, you may not believe that it can actually taste as good as it looks—but it does.

Actually, a lot of attention has been paid to eye appeal throughout the restaurant. When you first walk in, the room appears deceptively small. But as you continue inside, you will notice little nooks and crannies that are being used for dining space. Along one wall are several wooden booths with cano pies and signs. Most of the signs bear Spanish names such as Antonia, Carmen, Lucia, Carlos, Mario and Ricardo, but the sign hanging over the middle booth says: "Happiness is a warm tortilla."

The menu lists a variety of combination dinners that come with soup, refried beans and Spanish rice. The combinations offer various mixtures of tacos, tamales, enchiladas, tostadas and chiles rellenos. You may also order carne asada or chulupas (shredded chicken with green sauce and sour cream, topped with cheese and served on a tortilla). Other unusual entrees here are nopales con huevo (cactus, scramble with eggs and Spanish sauce), enchiladas de mole poblano (made with chicken, beef or cheese and topped with sour cream) and machaca (shredded bee marinated in sweet Spanish sauce and scrambled with eggs). *Magnificio!*

*1541 Taraval St., San Francisco; (415) 661-4929 &
50 West Portal Ave., San Francisco; (415) 664-9800
Sun. - Thurs. 11:30 - 9:00; Fri. - Sat. 11:30 - 10:00
Beer & wine
BA, MC
No reservations taken*

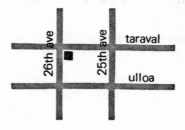

El Zarape Room

Mexican food seems to inspire less creativity in presentation than do many other types of cuisine. You probably wouldn't even realize this until you saw some of the beautifully prepared dishes at El Zarape Room.

While the food would be incredibly good anyway, the care taken at this little neighborhood restaurant makes everything seem even more delicious. The menu offers typical combination plates served atypic in enormous portions on platters about a foot and a half long.

Ordering the number one combo, which includes a fantastic chicken enchilada, chile relleno, taco, rice beans and salad, is a great way to experience the talent here. An even better way is to try one of the more unusual dishes, such as camarones rellenos (jumbo prawns filled with crabmeat and wrapped in bacon, served with fresh orange slices topped with maraschino cherries). This is the most expensive thin on the menu, and is served at many fine hotels for twice the price.

The food takes a little time to prepare and is brought to you piping hot. While you wait, enjoy a Bohemia beer and prepared yourself for a gastronomic odyssey.

3349 23rd St., San Francisco; (415) 824-9949
Sun. - Thurs. 10 - 8:30; Fri. & Sat. 10 - 2:00 a.m.
Beer & wine
No credit cards
Reservations advisable

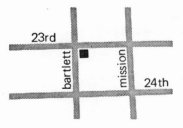

Hot House

You've got to like a Mexican restaurant that serves French sourdough bread with all orders and where everything on the menu is less than $3. Then there are the facts that the place has been in business since 1934, that many of its customers have been going there for at least 25 years, and that until that venerable amusement park was demolished in December 1972, it was located in Playland. So, nostalgia fans, this restaurant has everything going for it—including terrific food.

Tamales seem to be the specialty of the Hot House. You can order both old-fashioned beef tamales in husks and cup tamales, which are shaped like little chicken pies served upside down. The tacos are soft and rolled and served with a sauce that is actually like a Mexican gravy, rather than the typical Mexican hot sauce. (We were advised by one of the old-timers that you are supposed to dip the sourdough bread in the gravy.) Note: if you want refried beans with your meal, rather than ordinary beans, you must ask for them. There is also a lunch special that offers soup, salad, entree, dessert and a beverage for less than $2.

Obviously, the Hot House is a hot spot for good dining.

4052 Balboa St., San Francisco; (415) 386-9626
Sun. - Thurs. 11 - 10:30; Fri. & Sat. 11 - 11
Beer only
No credit cards
Reservations not taken

Mario's

From the number of signs in Mario's window, you might think he sold signs instead of great Mexican food. If you read the signs, at least you'll have some idea of what's in store. "Just Wonderful Mexican Food" it is. And it does have "Entertainment on Weekends 'Til 1 A.M."

Starting with the food (which is a good place to start at a restaurant), you will soon realize what a bargain Mario's is. Order any combination of three entrees from enchilada, taco, tamale or chile relleno and it will be served with fried beans, rice and salad. Or select the special dinner, which includes your choice of soup or salad, one of the above four entrees, rice, beans, tortillas, coffee and dessert. The only item we found disappointing was the chile relleno.

Mario's decor is fairly standard and reminds you of a Spanish vocabulary test: blankets, sombreros, masks, posters, bull horns, pinatas, candles, bandilleras (got you on that one—they're bullfighters' sticks) and velvet paintings. But they do brighten up the place.

If you have to leave San Francisco (and occasionally even the best people must make some sacrifices), don't forget to send a postcard back to Mario. He already has quite a collection pasted on the back wall.

900 Bush St., San Francisco; (415) 775-9604,
(415) 776-4490
Sun. - Thurs. 11:30 - 11; Fri. & Sat. 11 - 1
Beer & wine
MC
Reservations advisable

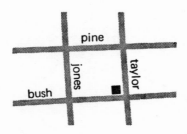

Roosevelt Tamale Parlor

The Roosevelt Tamale Parlor has been in the same location for more than 36 years, and it is hard to imagine why it has never been completely suffocated by lovers of great tamales. We mean really *great*, homemade, corn-husk tamales. Some fans *have* discovered it, and a line usually starts about 7 p.m. So either try an early dinner or stand in line. If you want conversation while you're standing, your best bet is to practice your Spanish.

Don't order more than you can eat unless you want to take it home. At the Roosevelt Tamale Parlor, they insist! But, if you don't mind, you might order the combination dinner: enchilada, tamale, taco, rice and beans. (Beware—that hot sauce is really hot, and we wouldn't want you to embarrass the other patrons of this tiny restaurant by screaming.)

There are few decorations (although the place should have been awarded some kind of medal for those great tamales) and no tablecloths. Actually, there are no frills of any kind. All the effort has been put into the food.

2817 24th St., San Francisco; (415) 648-9899
Tues. - Sun. 11 a.m. - 11 p.m.; closed Mon.
Beer only
No credit cards
Reservations advisable

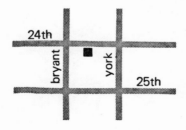

Tia Margarita

Considering the plethora of good Mexican restaurants found in Southern California, the scarcity of good Mexican restaurants in the Bay Area seems to be directly related to San Francisco's distance from California's southern border.

Of the few recommendable Mexican restaurants in the area, Tia Margarita is one of the most highly touted. The subtle, almost elegant decor provides an ideal setting for the delicious food, although it might mislead you into thinking that prices are higher than they really are. In fact, it is still a point of amazement that this lovely restaurant can serve such excellent food, so well prepared, at budget prices. But it does—and it has become famous for it.

There isn't a thing on the menu which can't be recommended, especially if you wash it down with one of the outstanding margaritas. Service is excellent, and the food is so beautifully presented that it seems almost a shame to disturb its symmetry. But with a huge taco, tostada or chile relleno tempting your fork, symmetry should be the last thing on your mind.

300 19th Ave. at Clement; San Francisco; (415) 752-9274
Mon. - Fri. 4 - 11; Sat. 4 - 11:30; Sun. 3 - 11
Full bar
No credit cards
Reservations advisable

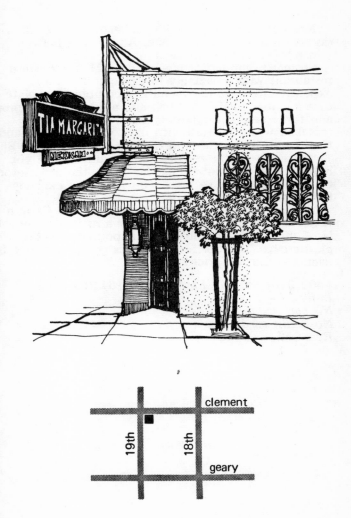

Cook 'n Baker

Not only does the Cook'n Baker sound like a donut shop, it looks like one. And its big plastic sign reinforces that impression.

Strangely enough, it is actually a Middle-Eastern restaurant with amazingly low prices. The most expensive item on the menu is a combination plate that includes falafel, kubbeh and a salad of cucumbe and tomatoes. The falafel is huge; the kubbeh (cracked wheat stuffed with meat and pine nuts and then fried) is terrific—and the price is well under $3.

There are Arabic records on the jukebox. If you have trouble understanding the lyrics, the proprietors may be persuaded to teach you Arabic in exchange for English lessons.

Tucked away in the Mission District, the Cook'n Baker is obviously not a place for a night on the tow No liquor is served and coffee is poured into disposa plastic cups. But the food really is good, everyone is friendly, and the prices are right.

3200 24th St., San Francisco; (415) 285-7861
Daily 11 - 9
No bar
No credit cards
Reservations advisable

Marrakech Express

There are basically two kinds of Middle-Eastern
restaurants: the kind where you are transformed
into a character out of the Arabian nights and the
kind that resembles a shish-kebab assembly line.
The food at both is usually about the same,
although the quality may vary, and the prices
generally reflect the different amounts spent
on overhead.

Marrakech Express in Berkeley is a fine example
of the latter genre. While it offers a variety of shish
kebabs and kebab sandwiches, it also has a few salads
and falafel. For the uninitiated, falafel is a kind of
Middle-Eastern taco and consists of a small round
loaf of pita bread stuffed with lettuce, tomatoes
and deep-fried "meatballs" made of ground gar-
banzo beans, spices and vegetables. Usually this
is topped with a sesame-seed sauce, but unfortunately
at Marrakech Express it seems to be topped with
salad dressing. Other than this, it is a great treat
and very filling.

The kebabs are tasty, made of good quality meat
and served with onions, rice and feta cheese. The
cheese is also found in quantity on the delicious
dinner salad.

There are both indoor and outdoor dining
areas, and the service consists of the waiter bring-
ing your food, a pile of paper napkins and a collection
of utensils. So if you really like to be waited on, it's
off to the fancy tents and pillows on the floor—and
higher prices.

1839 Euclid Ave., Berkeley; (415) 848-4370
Daily 11 - 10
Beer & wine
No credit cards
Reservations advisable

Tycoon

Tycoon is a place where you'd gladly splurge, but you don't need to. That, indeed, is the philosoph of the owners of this beautiful restaurant: You don't have to be a tycoon to feel like one.

And they do make you feel like one. The owners are the three Vartan brothers—two are architects and one is a civil engineer. They have applied their training and expertise to creating a spectacular dining environment. From the thick, rust-colored shag rug to the central sculpture—a creation of palm fronds and grapevines by a Japanese flower-arranging master—the decor is relaxing and inviting.

The menu offers only about eight entrees, including fish Mediterranean, chicken sevan and koufta a la ourpha. The latter is particularly interesting— ground meat and cracked wheat formed into balls, skewered with chunks of stuffed eggplant and served on a bed of rice. The dinner includes an appetizer plate with pieces of pita bread and vegetables to be dunked in indescribable but delicious sauces. Also included are soup or salad and dessert. All this is yours for around $5.

Tycoon is a true find, and one that we are most excited about sharing with you.

4012 Geary Blvd. at 4th Ave., San Francisco
  (415) 387-9600
Open 6 days 5 - 10; closed Tues.
Wine only
No credit cards
Reservations advisable

Bernini's

Bernini's is actually Bernini's International Coffee House, but it is a delightful restaurant, too. One of the most striking things about Bernini's is its exterior which has been completely covered with a collage made up of pieces of wood. It blends in beautifully with the brick chimney in front, and the entire old house has taken on a new and inviting personality.

Great salads, fruit, cheese, bread and wine are standard fare at Bernini's. Ask for a table on the patio, where you can admire the architecture and the local crowd that passes on its way to or from Telegraph Avenue. On a sunny afternoon or twilit evening, with a terrific crab salad—or maybe a sandwich board from which you can create an appetizing concoction—Bernini's is the best place to be in the East Bay.

2511 Channing Way, Berkeley; (415) 849-0734
Mon. - Thurs. 11 - 11:30; Fri. & Sat. 11 - 12:30;
   Sun. 11 - 11:30
Beer & wine
No credit cards
Reservations advisable

BERKELEY

The Haven

The Salvation Army depot or local rescue mission are still good places to go if you're wandering the streets at night hungry.

However, if you're wandering because you can't find a place that's open and serving good food, seek and ye shall find the Haven (no, it's not a religious sanctuary).

In addition to being open 24 hours a day, the Haven has other outstanding features: huge salads, delicious sandwiches served on nine-grain bread, and terrific omelettes served with fresh fruit. The orientation is "healthy," which means meal-sized portions, a lot of alfalfa sprouts and fresh ingredients. It is a cafeteria-style affair decorated with old-fashioned brass lanterns, colorful vintage pictures and stained-glass windows. The mood is mellow and one of good-food appreciation.

It really is a haven for the hungry—at anytime of day or night.

Polk St. at California St., San Francisco: (415)
474-3930
Open 24 hours
Beer & wine
No credit cards
No reservations taken

Shandygaff

Eating at Shandygaff makes you wonder why so many everyday food items are prepared with artificial aids when the food here, prepared without them, tastes so fresh and good. For the full "spiel," read the Shandygaff menu, which explains why the restaurant serves natural foods and describes the ingredients in many of its staple items.

When you first see Shandygaff, with the name of the restaurant written in huge letters that wrap around two sides of the building, it seems almost cold-looking. Inside, however, bright colors are dominant, with green and white walls and a red ceiling from which are hung silver tubular rods holding large, bright banners. There are fresh flowers on the tables.

The food is truly fine. Omelettes, spectacular salads, special sandwiches on delicious bread, pasta made from whole wheat and soybeans, and desserts all taste as if they had been thoughtfully and carefully prepared. It's amazing how ingredients which are so good individually can be put together into unusual and exciting combinations.

Consideration for the individual is very evident here. There are special salads for dieters and special sandwiches for children (of all ages). And no smoking is allowed in the restaurant.

1760 Polk St., San Francisco; (415) 441-1760
Mon. - Thurs. 12 - 10; Fri. & Sat. 12 - 11
Wine only
No credit cards
No reservations taken

Trident

This restaurant looks as if it was born in a puff of smoke from a genie's bottle. And I couldn't even try to tell you what that genie was smoking.

Overlooking the water in Sausalito, the Trident is furnished like the interior of some dream vessel. Ferns and tie-dyed velvet swags hang from the ceiling. Ivy clings to the walls and sunlight filters in through skylights. Polished wood gleams from the floor, walls and tables. Murals decorate the ceiling and walls. From the inside, you can sit surrounded by this living decor and glance out to the bay and the San Francisco skyline. Or you can dine in the sun on the outside deck and wave to the ships that seem close enough to throw you a lifeline.

The food is as varied as the decor. Casseroles, steaks, salads, waffles, eggs, sandwiches, homemade soups and lots more are all tempting. The menu claims that the restaurant tries to serve "good tasting, natural, wholesome, chemically free foods in a living, growing, stimulating atmosphere." It has indeed succeeded.

At the Trident, our special recommendations run the gamut from teriyaki steak to the super salads to the Trident Health Shake—a rich, delicious organic blending of yogurt, honey, fresh fruit and wheat germ.

Parking here is unfortunately a problem. It costs $.50 an hour at the restaurant, and several enjoyable hours can easily be spent there. If the extra fare is going to hurt your budget, allow yourself time to search for a space on a side street.

558 Bridgeway Blvd., Sausalito; (415) 332-1334
Daily 11 - 2 a.m.; closed Mon.
Full bar
No credit cards
No reservations taken

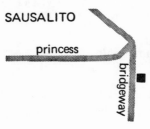

Warszawa

If everyone could dine at Warszawa, it would for-
ever put an end to Polish jokes. The food here is
obviously prepared with such care and attention
that the resulting dishes could make an interna-
tionalist of even the most hard-nosed bigot.

Enough philosophy; let's get down to the basics.
Warszawa is located in a converted house on a corner
in Berkeley. If you could find a time when it wasn't
busy, you might be able to appreciate dining in
the living room on such good homemade food. As
it is, the place is usually crowded, so you lose sight
of the atmospheric potential.

There are only six entrees, priced reasonably
enough so that the *a la carte* menu doesn't put you
off. These include (and I won't even try to write
them in Polish—there's something frightening about
all those consonants lumped together): beef and
mushrooms in sour-cream sauce with homemade egg
noodles; slices of beef rolled up around bacon and
vegetables; stuffed cabbage; traditional Polish hunter's
stew; crepes stuffed with meat and mushrooms; and
a combination plate of small ravioli-like pastries filled
with meat, cheese and mushrooms.

The appetizers are excellent, especially the herring
in sour cream and the cold borscht. Dessert must
be cheesecake.

1549 Shattuck Ave., Berkeley; (415) 841-5539
Wed. - Mon. 5 - 10; closed Tues.
Beer & wine
No credit cards
Reservations advisable

Tiburon Tommie's Mai Tai

Good Polynesian food accompanied by the shimmering rhythms of the ocean results in a feast for all the senses. And in the overcommercialized setting of Tiburon, a reasonably priced menu is paradise in itself. So a restaurant with all these features is truly special. Tiburon Tommie's offers all this; and while the ideal way to reach this enjoyable spot would be by outrigger canoe, we suggest that you try it even if you can't find your paddles.

Here you can dine on traditional Polynesian delicacies such as mandarin duck and those special Polynesian spare ribs. Or you can venture into the more exotic with celestial chicken (breast of chicken cutlets rolled in water chestnut mixture, simmered in peanut oil, served with mushroom and sprinkled with sesame seeds) or oyster filet of beef (sliced filet of tenderloin, seasoned and simmered in oyster sauce).

If you have 35 friends, you can really go overboard and get a complete Tahitian feast for only $15 per person. Otherwise, try this delightful cuisine with just one close friend and take advantage of the romantic atmosphere created by the island-oriented decor, the reflection of the stars on the ocean and the superb food. Even the service makes you feel that you're experiencing a special evening.

Pier 31, Tiburon; (415) 435-1229
Mon. - Sat. 11:30 - 10:45; Sun. 11:30 - 9:45
Full bar
AE, BA, MC
Reservations advisable

TIBURON

beach

tiburon

main

Miniature Russian

If you don't succumb to the bakery smell and dive headlong into a row of fresh pastries, you'll be in for a special dinner treat at the Miniature Russian restaurant. Unfortunately, you must walk through the bakery to get to the dining room, and many good intentions have not survived that journey.

Once you've successfully completed that perilous trek, however, prepare yourself for some of the most authentic and savory Russian cooking in this city. Fine creations such as beef stroganoff, schnitzel, cabbage rolls and veal or lamb roast are served here regularly. One of the most interesting dishes is the zrazl—a Russian hamburger with stuffing. The Miniature is also patronized by people who come just for soups: borscht, kidney soup, barley soup and spinach soup.

Complete dinners include soup, salad, coffee and dessert, so you'll get to try a lot of everything good. Weibel wines are available and are stacked in the rear of the restaurant in what looks like a butcher's meat display case. Our only reservation about the Miniature is that we were charged for our second cups of coffee.

433 Clement St., San Francisco; (415) 752-4444
Daily 8 - 8; closed Mon.
No bar
No credit cards
Reservations advisable

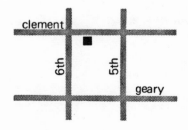

Arne's Cedar Lane Cellar

Cedar Lane is more of an alley than a lane, but this hasn't kept Arne's reputation from spreading so rapidly that he just expanded his restaurant all the way through to Geary. This Scandinavian delicatessen and restaurant claims on its front window that inside you will find "food to be enjoyed—quiet, delightful atmosphere . . . or to take home or for pleasure."

While the prices here are currently very reasonable Arne also has a sign posted inside which warns: "Prices subject to change while eating." (We paid exactly what the menu stated, however.) Dinners offered included an interesting selection of entrees, including Norwegian fish balls, old-fashioned beef stew, fried turbot and kielbasa (Polish sausage) mit kraut. The highest-priced dinner was a 14-ounce New York cut sirloin for under $5. Domestic and importe beer, aperitifs and champagne are also available, and all go very well with Arne's sandwiches and salads.

Arne's signs also claim that the restaurant is "the original house of danick frekadeller;" and if we knew what that was, maybe we could recommend it, too.

127 Cedar Lane, San Francisco; (415) 441-0934
Daily 11 - 11
Beer & wine
No credit cards
No reservations taken

Arne's

post

van ness   polk   cedar

geary

Butler's Pantry

A small unknown restaurant in Tiburon which serves delicious food at reasonable prices simply can't remain unknown for long. We can only hope that it will maintain the quality of its food and its delightful atmosphere without succumbing to the urge to match typical Tiburon tariffs.

Butler's Pantry (and we hope they put a sign outside soon) is just such a spot. The triangular dining room holds six small tables, and yellow and white checked curtains flutter at the windows.

The menu consists of special Norwegian dinners such as Norwegian meatballs, bratwurst, roast pork, islandic fried herring, baked chicken, etc. The meatballs are especially delicious and are served with cabbage, a potato-and-cheese side dish, peas, lingonberries and whole-wheat bread.

If you're not in the mood for a complete dinner, try one of the super sandwiches (the Viking burger is outstanding) or one of the delicate omelettes. The Butler's Special Omelette with shrimp, sour cream, chives and tomatoes is excellent. And each omelette is served with a piece of fresh fruit. The hot wine and fruit gloggs here are perfect and will complement any dinner choice.

Tiburon Blvd. and Juanita Lane, Tiburon;
(415) 789-9877
Tues. - Sun. 11 - 9; closed Mon.
Beer & wine
No credit cards
Reservations advisable

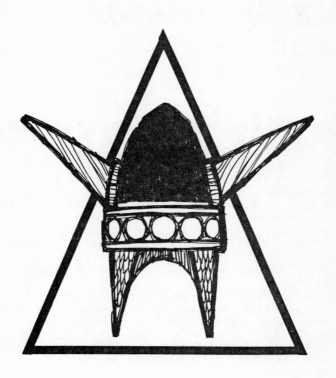

TIBURON

Einer's Danish Fondue

This is the only place in town that specializes in Danish food for dinner. The food is excellent and inexpensive; the atmosphere can be whatever you want to make it.

As you look around, you can see the possibilities: you can opt for an intimate dinner with soft yellow lights and mood music on the stereo; or you can gather a group around the long wooden table beside a bookcase that looks as though it has been transplanted from your own home complete with magazines, books, dishes and that old rock collection you've been meaning to throw out; or you can perch upon a stool at the wooden bar and drink German or Danish beer and play chess or checkers; or, finally, you can engage in a game of English darts and keep score on the blackboard hanging nearby.

Once you know what you're doing, try the København-hauner bøf (Copenhagen beef): ground sirloin mixed with onions and spices and set on bread and lightly fried. This is served either with capers, garnish and raw egg yolk, or with sauteed mushrooms. We also recommend the hytte pølsemad (cottage sausage feed), a delicious ham sausage served with cottage-fried potatoes and an ample supply of pickled beets. A couple can enjoy a cheese fondue made with select Danish cheese and served with bread cubes and roasted sesame seeds. Old-timers usually stick to the Danish smørrebrød, consisting of a variety of fish, meats and cheeses in a colorful arrangement.

1901 Clement St., San Francisco; (415) 386-9860
Daily 6 - 11
Beer & wine
No credit cards
No reservations taken

The Cove

The best time to go to the Cove is on a Friday night when you're not in a hurry. This is because several of its dinners are offered only on Friday nights, and because the menu notes that there is a 30-minute wait for a few other selections. (At least they warn you.)

While the Cove serves Italian specialties such as pastas, minestrone, chicken cacciatore and veal parmesan, it also offers abalone steak, pot roast, liver and onions, and cheeseburgers. Some of the most interesting dinners include vongole (spaghetti with clams—lots of clams) and maritata (Italian wedding soup). The lasagne is also particularly good, with a thick sauce and a composition that doesn't collapse into a noodle casserole the minute you touch it with a fork. A relish tray starts off the meal with cheese, carrots, celery, salami, olives and green peppers. Soup or salad is extra, but the nonpasta entrees are served with pasta or vegetables. The food is steaming hot and tastes freshly prepared.

Not bad for a place that used to be a laundry.

4401 Balboa St., San Francisco; (415) 752-2422
Daily 4 - 12
Beer & wine
No credit cards
Reservations advisable

Crab Cottage

OK, so if the specialty of your restaurant was abalone, you'd call it the Abalone Alcove instead of the Crab Cottage. Well, Tom Monaghan, the man who owns this restaurant and dives for the red abalone must have his reasons. Maybe he resents the abalone because he has to use an abalone iron to pry them from their undersea ledges, where they cling with a suction power of up to 1,500 pounds per square inch. If he does resent them, he hides it very well, because the abalone here is the most tender and tasty we've had in the Bay Area.

This is definitely a place for fish freaks. The only item on the menu that isn't from under the sea is one lonely hamburger sandwich. And everything here is extraordinary, from the crab sandwich to the fried oysters to the steamed clams to the fried prawns and scallops. And, of course, the abalone.

The restaurant itself is charming, though simple. There's a white picket fence in front of the blue building with its blue and white awning. The service is friendly and conscientious, and there are fresh flowers on the tables. Princeton Bay is a delightful spot, and the prospect of dining at the Crab Cottage will encourage you to visit there often.

On Capistrano Rd. at Prospect Way, Princeton-by-
the-Sea
Wed. - Sun. 12 - 9; closed Mon. & Tues.
Beer only
BA, MC
No reservations taken

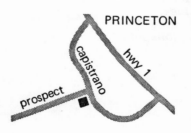

Ernie's Neptune Fish Grotto

This is not the kind of place where you can dine on seafood while you listen to the waves breaking. The only thing breaking here will be your will power, and the noises you hear will be those of satisfied diners and street traffic.

This is a plain little restaurant with a prominent counter and some tables, all laden with Ernie's delicious creations. Baked and poached fish are very special here, and the sauces complement the seafood flavors perfectly. Both the Coney Island and Boston clam chowders swim with chunks of clams; no fillers, such as potatoes, are used to thicken the rich soups. The salads are also outstanding, especially the shrimp and crab louies, which are heaped high with meat. Shrimp and crab omelettes are also available. Side dishes include fresh sourdough bread and thick, crisp fries.

The waitresses here really hustle, but the service is friendly and efficient. Since Ernie's has been established for 40 years, the staff has really had time to get everything down perfectly.

1816 Irving St., San Francisco; (415) 566-3344
Tues. - Thurs. 11 - 9; Fri. 11 - 10; Sat & Sun. 4 - 9;
*   closed Mon.*
Beer & wine
No credit cards
No reservations taken

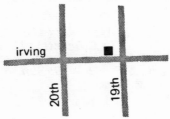

La Bouillabaisse

La Bouillabaisse is a French seafood restaurant (with a fish market in the next room) that regards seafood as a sculptor regards clay—something to be molded into an artistic creation. It's one of those places where you want to try everything on the menu. Once you taste one dish, you may even return often enough to do just that.

The La Bouillabaisse menu distinguishes between "Real Bouillabaisse from Marseilles" and "Cioppino French Style," claiming that the two dishes are often confused. The "Real Bouillabaisse" is defined as a stew of whole fish such as salmon, sea bass, halibut, tuna, clams and jumbo shrimp in a broth spiced with saffron and served with Aioli homemade dressing. Cioppino, on the other hand, contains fish in the shell (such as crab, shrimp, scallops and lobster) and is made with tomato, sauce and spices. They are both superb here, and you *can* taste the difference.

Other entrees include fresh oyster casserole, coquille St. Jacques, trout, frog legs, abalone and a variety of pan-fried fish. You absolutely must try the onion soup, made with domestic Swiss cheese.

La Bouillabaisse seems full of life, with red and white checks on the tablecloths, red roses on the wallpaper, candles on the tables and bustling waiters. But its obvious reverence for good seafood is the best indication of the restaurant's appreciation of the good life.

2424 Lincoln Ave., Alameda; (415) 521-8844
"Under the bridge" in Crockett; (415) 787-9933
Lunch: Wed. - Fri. 11 - 2, Dinner Wed. - Thurs.
  5 - 9:30; Fri. & Sat. 5 - 10; Sun. 5 - 9;
  closed Mon. & Tues.
Beer & wine
MC
Reservations advisable

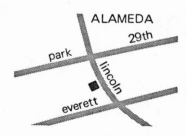

Maye's Oyster House

There are so many good things to order at Maye's that you could spend most of your time here just deciding what you want to try first. Of course, if you're fond of clams or oysters, this is the best place to order them when they're in season; otherwise, the entrees are seemingly endless.

Complete dinners include soup du jour; choice of salad, tomato juice or seafood cocktail; pasta with mushroom sauce; dessert; and coffee or tea. Our chowder was thick and delicious, the seafood cocktail was accompanied by a nice sauce, the salad had a good house dressing poured over strips of beets, carrots, tomatoes and lettuce, and we found the soft noodles very tasty. Also included with the meal were sourdough bread and wholewheat crackers. The rice custard, unfortunately, was a little drab.

Portions are huge and everyone seems to enjoy himself. Many customers have been coming here for years because they know they can count on the quality of the food. The restaurant seats about a hundred and there's usually not more than a ten-minute wait. Maye's is simply a pleasantly unpretentious place with great seafood dinners.

1233 Polk St., San Francisco; (415) 474-7674
Daily 11 - 10:30
Full bar
No credit cards
Reservations advisable

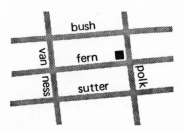

Pier 29

Steak and seafood restaurants located on the ocean often take advantage of their romantic atmosphere to skimp on the quality of the food. So it is indeed a pleasure to recommend a steak and seafood restaurant that prizes quality and good service along with the charms of its marine atmosphere.

Pier 29, on the pier in Oakland, fits the latter description perfectly. Dining at a hatch-cover table while looking at the view is indeed enjoyable here. And so is the food. Steak, seafood or combination dinners are served with a chilled tossed green salad, Idaho baked potato or french fries. The salad has a nice Italian dressing and includes fresh shrimp. Steaks are thick, tender and beautifully cooked to order. The kitchen is out in the open and you can see and hear the steaks sizzling over the flames in the barbecue pit.

Pier 29 is, however, a very popular place, and the decibel level reflects this. So don't expect a serene, romantic atmosphere. Just anticipate a delicious dinner and you won't be disappointed.

300 29th Ave., Alameda; (415) 261-1621
Lunch: Sun. - Fri. 11:30 - 2:30; Sat. 12 - 2:30;
  dinner 5 - 10 daily
Full bar
AE, BA, MC
Reservations advisable

ALAMEDA

Sand Dollar

The drive to Stinson Beach can be beautifully scenic or a little nerve-racking—depending on whether or not you take the curvy route. Either way, the prospect of dining at the Sand Dollar provides ample reason for making the trip.

Try to imagine a cozy little place on the beach serving steaks, chops and seafood where half the items on the menu are less than $5. Imagine swinging doors opening into a room with 14 to 16 tables, courteous service and a relaxing atmosphere. Now imagine fantastic fish, always fresh and delicious, or big, tender steaks, juicy and flavorful. If your imagination isn't salivating by now, try the homemade vegetable soup loaded with tomatoes, onions, mushrooms and other garden varietals.

If it sounds tempting—well, it is. After your drive (and it really is lovely), relax on the porch of the Sand Dollar with one of its generous drinks. Maybe take a peek at its extensive wine list. Then enjoy a fine meal comfortably, without being rushed and without large crowds. Could we give you anything more?

Highway 1 Stinson Beach (just before stop sign),
(415) 868-0434
Fri. 6 - 10 p.m.; Sat. 5:30 - 10 p.m.; Sun.
5:30 - 9:30 p.m.; weekdays 6 - 8 p.m. (varies
call for exact times); closed Jan. & Feb.
Full bar
No credit cards
Reservations advisable

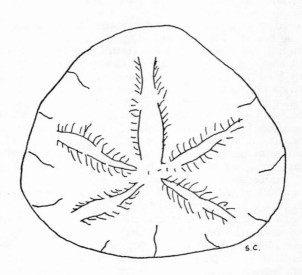

S.C.

calle del mar

shoreline

belvedere

STINSON
BEACH

Scoma's

By hook or by crook, you're eventually going to get to Fisherman's Wharf. And while you won't find a restaurant there that isn't overrun with tourists, Scoma's is just a little bit out of the way and the place many natives prefer. It may be crowded and you will undoubtedly have to wait to be seated, for the dining space is actually a much smaller part of the restaurant than it appears. But there is a lovely view of moored fishing boats, and a boisterous bar where you can pass the time.

The menu has a fine selection of seafood, a few steaks and pasta dishes, salads and some sandwiches. To give you an example of its scope, you can get a shrimp Louis salad, a shrimp sandwich, scampi, prawns sauteed with a bordelaise sauce or french-fried prawns. If you're not in the mood for shrimp, you can order abalone, crab, sole, rock cod, calamari, sand dabs, mahi mahi, frog legs, scallops, oysters, cioppino or, of course, lobster. Prices hover around $5; many items are less, and a few are higher.

The Scoma brothers claim that their restaurant represents the *real* Fisherman's Wharf, and they have planned their multilevel establishment to be as different as possible from the glass and wood structures typical of the Wharf. They have done a fine job on a difficult project. When you're at the Wharf, this is the best place to dine.

Pier 47 - Foot of Jones St. at Jefferson St., San Francisco; (415) 771-4383
Open daily 11:30 - 11:30
Full bar
AE, BA, MC
No reservations taken

jefferson

jones

7 Seas

The 7 Seas restaurant is a great place for a sea-food break in the visually delightful town of Sausalito. And if you're the kind that worries about the cleanliness of restaurant kitchens, you can set your mind at ease after walking through the kitchen here to reach the patio dining area in back.

This garden dining area with its ivy-covered walls is perfect for enjoying delicious prawns curry or prawns au berre—two unusual dishes served in a tasty cream sauce. Or, if you're more the indoor type, you can dine on such delightful delicacies as bouillabaisse, sole marguery, mahi mahi or crab romano in the dining area next to the bar. A small green salad is included with your meal.

The 7 Seas is a casual restaurant and more quiet and cozy than are most in Sausalito. In the evening, the indoor dining area is softly illuminated and the garden area is flooded with red and white lights. There is only room for about 45 diners, and if you're one of the lucky few, you'll have discovered a fine spot for enjoying the bounty of the sea.

682 Bridgaway Blvd, Sausalito; (415) 332-1304
Daily 11:30 - 11:30
Full bar
AE, BA, MC
Reservations advisable

Spenger's

Well, with the quality of seafood served in restaurants ranging from indigestible to incredibly delicious, you know you're going to have to sacrifice something for consistently excellent seafood at reasonable prices. At Spenger's, what is sacrificed is atmosphere—unless, of course, you can feel romantic in seemingly endless dining halls, surrounded by hundreds of other diners who are all looking around as if they're afraid they'll lose their places at the tables.

But if your only concern is good seafood, pshaw on all the missing frills. Here you can order anything from the vast menu and be assured of its quality. In fact, if the hustle and bustle upset you, you can order anything on the menu to go.

Try staying once just to experience what restaurant success can mean. While you wait to be seated (and you will), you can throw down a few at the huge bar. (Take it easy, or your lobster will taste pickled.)

This may all sound discouraging, but if handled with a spirit of fun and a sense of appreciation for the still-low prices, you will enjoy yourself and probably even come back. Because it really isn't worth paying two or three times the price for unreliable seafood somewhere else.

1919 Fourth St., Berkeley; (415) 845-7771
Daily 8 a.m. - midnight
Full bar
AE, BA, MC
Reservations advisable

Spencer's Fish Grotto

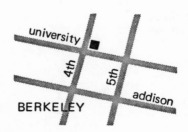

university

4th

5th

addison

BERKELEY

The Beginning

OK, sports fans. So you want to know how Nate Thurmond got to be that big. Well, if you ate the kind of good food he serves at his soul food restaurant every day, you might grow, too. Not necessarily upward—but, for sure, outward.

This is soul food good for anybody's soul. Out-of-this-world Southern fried chicken, barbecued spareribs like your back-yard barbecue never saw, pot roast, gumbo, rib eye steak—all great. Dinners include either soup or salad, corn bread, dessert and your choice of two vegetables of the day from such possibilities as mustard greens, black-eyed peas, rice, mashed potatoes, string beans and corn. On Sunday, there are also hot biscuits—light, crusty and incredibly good.

The place is pretty busy on Friday and Saturday nights, but if Nate's there (and he's around a lot when he's not playing basketball), he'll make you feel at home. The interior is warm and inviting, with a big stove in the center of the room and old well buckets enclosing the ceiling lights.

One thing for sure—you gotta try the sweet-potato pie for dessert.

2020 Fillmore St., San Francisco; (415) 567-9948
Tues. - Thurs. 11 - 11; Fri. & Sat. 11 - 12;
closed Mon.
Full bar
No credit cards
No reservations taken

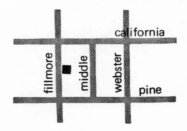

Pabellón Español

Paella fans—this is the place. Walk into Pabellon Espanol, order the paella a la valenciana and in 20 minutes you will have an iron kettle full of rice, crab, prawns, clams, squid, cod, ham, sausage and chicken. This is a literal treasure trove with moist, flavorful rice and more pieces of fish and meat than you've probably ever seen before in a paella.

The complete dinner includes a salad with peas, lettuce and carrots topped by a nice house dressing, plus large hot, buttered dinner rolls. Other good things on the menu range from rack of lamb to a gaucho steak, although seafood is the specialty.

The restaurant is small, with a bar to one side and flamenco guitar entertainment Friday and Saturday nights from 9 to 11 p.m. it is a most pleasant place to dine and the menu and food are both exciting. In order not to mislead you, the amount of time necessary for preparation is stated along with each menu item. If you're lucky, you may even be offered a free taste of the special of the day. We encourage you to take advantage.

3115 22nd St., San Francisco; (415) 824-9852
Mon., Wed., Thurs. 4 - 11; Fri. & Sat. 12- 4 a.m.;
Sun. 12 - 11; closed Tues.
Beer & wine
No credit cards
No reservations taken

Cordon Bleu

Five-spice chicken at the Cordon Bleu is one of those wonders that make dining out so exciting. The recipe is a secret, but at approximately $2 for half a chicken, you don't need to learn how to make it at home. In fact, for what it will cost you to enjoy a fine meal of Vietnamese food at the Cordon Bleu, it almost doesn't pay to eat at home at all.

Here you can start your meal with an imperial roll for less than $1. While it looks like a standard egg roll, it is stuffed with meat, vegetables, mushrooms and bean thread, rolled in "rice paper" and dipped in a light sauce. The sauce has a mild, mild fish base, garlic, lemon and other good things that really complement the flavor of the roll. From there you can proceed to a superb won ton soup, the five-spice chicken and other additions of your choice. Combination dinners are also available.

If you're hesitant to explore the *a la carte* menu on your own, just ask the gracious hostess to point you in the right direction. The service here is prompt and courteous, and enhances the quiet atmosphere in the one-room restaurant.

This is not a fancy place, and the decorations consist mainly of coolie hats made into lamps. But the prices reflect the lack of ostentation, making you think about what you're really paying for at other restaurants.

2227 Polk St., San Francisco; (415) 441-7187;
1574 California St., San Francisco; (415) 673-5637
Tues. - Thurs. 5 - 10; Fri. & Sat. 5 - 11; closed Mon.
Beer & wine
BA, MC
Reservations advisable

Thanh Long

Authenticity is so important to the owners of Thanh Long (Green Dragon) Vietnamese restaurant that the rau ram herb is flown in specially from Vietnam in order to season the food perfectly. And perfect seasoning—as well as perfect preparation—is typical of all the food here.

House specialties reflect this kind of care and attention. Roast crab, offered as an appetizer but sufficient as an entree for two, is composed of a whole live crab fully baked, then roasted with butter and spices—tremendous! Cha gio, another specialty, is made of ten ground ingredients: meat (veal, beef or pork), shrimp, crab, chicken, egg yolk, soybean sprout, mushroom, onion, carrot and white vermicelli, all wrapped in rice paper. It tastes as good as it sounds. Several of the combination dinners include cha gio, along with soup, rice and another main dish. American dishes and sandwiches are also available, but ordering those would be like going to Paris and then staying in your hotel room to watch TV.

4101 Judah St. at 46th Ave., San Francisco;
(415) 665-1146
Tues. - Sun. 11:30 - 9 p.m.; closed Mon.
Beer & wine
No credit cards
Reservations advisable

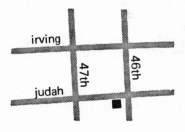

Vietnam-France

Despite its name, this restaurant is predominantly Vietnamese and offers only three French dinners. Twenty complete Vietnamese dinners are also available, and each is exceptionally good. The main ingredient in the dinners is usually beef, pork or chicken, served with vegetables, although specialties such as pork-and-prawn brochette are also offered.

Four dishes, each of which must be ordered in advance for a minimum of four persons, sound particularly enticing. Although we did not try them, they are: beef in seven styles, Vietnamese fondue, salt-and-pepper fried crab and charcoal-broiled fish a la Hanoi. The combination dinner—which includes Vietnamese pork shish kebab, imperial rolls filled with pork, shrimp, mushroom and vegetables, and rice topped with a tasty sauce—is also very good.

Soup is included in the price of dinner. Ours was a thick chicken-rice concoction that tasted delicious. Available wines include Mondavi, Krug, Almaden and Jadot.

Wood paneling, green and yellow checked tablecloths and a few strategically placed plants contribute to the sunny feeling in this small restaurant. It's also a good place to try for lunch.

1901 Divisadero St., San Francisco; (415) 563-9575
Mon. - Thurs. 11 - 2, 5 - 10; Fri. & Sat. 11 - 2,
*   5 - 10:30; closed Sun.*
Beer & wine
No credit cards
Reservations advisable

Buena Vista

The Buena Vista is one of those San Francisco institutions that you just shouldn't miss. In fact, whatever you're looking for in San Francisco you'll probably find at the BV.

Famous for its Irish coffee, the BV caters largely to a crowd that goes there for drinking and dallying and admiring the beautiful view of the bay. These patrons are usually young, single and gregarious, and during an evening's time you can expect a number of friendships to develop. Aside from its well-deserved reputation as a place to go to meet people, however, the BV also serves breakfasts and dinners at remarkably reasonable prices. For around $3, you can dine on pot roast, beef enchilada, breaded veal cutlet, pan-fried chicken, grilled steak sandwich, curried shrimp or smoked oysters. And the food is good—not spectacular, but good.

Because of the ever-present crowd at the BV, the best way to get a table is to give your name to a waitress who will then scout around for you. In addition to the tables in the bar area, there is also a small dining room in back. But don't think that by sitting down you're going to miss any of the action. Someone you don't know will probably be seated at your table very shortly, either because there's no more room elsewhere or because his or her feet hurt.

2765 Hyde St. at Beach St., San Francisco
  (415) 474-5044
Daily 9 a.m. - 2 a.m.
Full bar
No credit cards
No reservations taken

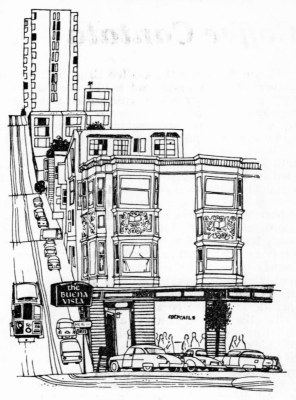

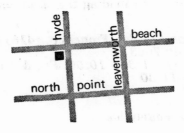

Coffee Cantata

Please don't try the Coffee Cantata if you're in a hurry, for the restaurant is like one big, over-stuffed easy chair where you should relax and simply enjoy your surroundings. Plants here seem to grow without encouragement, as if they liked clinging to the paneled walls. A fresh rosebud nestles in a small vase on each of the ceramic tile tables. Exciting wood sculptures and oil paintings also fit beautifully into a mood enhanced by the classical melodies piped into the restaurant.

It is hard to accept that a restaurant offering international dishes can actually succeed in present-ing them all well. But at the Coffee Cantata, every-thing from the curried chicken to the carnitas is superior. The food is prepared with the same pride that is evident in the restaurant's decor. Meat and poultry are of superior quality and flavor; side dishes are distinctive and delicious. Full dinners include salad, coffee and dessert.

Try the curried chicken as an introduction to this fine restaurant. You will discover huge chunks of chicken in a just-right sauce, along with heaps of coconut, peanuts, chutney, pilaf and raisins. The herbal dressing on the salad and the German chocolate cake are also highly recommended. The coffee is a special blend and is rich and inviting. Since portions are very generous, you might even order just one complete dinner (dividing the salad and cake) for two people.

2030 Union St., San Francisco; (415) 931-0770,
(415) 930-7043
Sun. - Thurs. 11:30 - 10:00; Fri. & Sat.
11:30 - 11:30
Full bar
BA, MC
Reservations advisable

coffee cantata

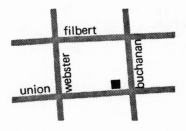

Family Farmacy

Don't go to the Family Farmacy if you get up-tight easily. Besides the unusual and unconventional people who frequent this spot, it's a sit-on-a-pillow-on-the-floor affair. (If you arrive after 9 p.m., it's time-to-listen-to-local-talent, which is sometimes very good.) The tables are old telephone cable spools, the walls are covered with redwood bark, and faded tie-dyed coverings hang from the ceiling. The only word for the atmosphere is "funky."

However, if you're starving and almost broke, you can eat all you want for about a dollar on Tuesdays (spaghetti with mushroom sauce), Wednesdays (tuna casserole) and Thursdays (split-pea soup and tossed salad). We didn't try the spaghetti, but the tuna casserole will fill you up and provide nutrition pleasantly. The pea soup is kind of blah.

If you've got a few more coins, try one of the super sandwiches. They are served on brown bread that tastes like ambrosia with a thick layer of ham, cheese, salami or peanut butter. This incredible bread is also served by itself warm with butter. The homemade chocolate cake is also a good buy: the chocolate is rich, the cake is moist and the slice weighs about a quarter of a pound.

4344 California St., San Francisco; (415) 668-7755
Daily 11 a.m. - 1:30 a.m.
No bar
No credit cards, but will take food stamps
No reservations taken

Fanny's

A visit to Fanny's is a nostalgia trip that will remind you of what the good old days were supposed to have been like. The menus are all encased in old sheet music and the brownish walls are hung with '20s-style art. The balcony holds several white wicker dining tables. The dishes are fussily floral and unmatched. The food is also unmatched.

The menu includes early California specialties, omelettes, salads and miscellaneous good things. We highly recommend the beef stroganoff, which is laden with a creamy sauce chock full of tender beef cubes and mushrooms. Another special treat here is the California toast—raisin nut French toast hidden under mounds of fresh strawberries, grapes, apples, oranges and cantaloupe. Dinner includes an antipasto vegetable plate and delicious homemade vegetable soup, plus fresh vegetables. For dessert, try the spectacular cheesecake.

The service here is excellent—the waiters literally dash up and down the stairs in order to keep things moving at an appropriate pace. Altogether, a great spot.

4230 18th St., San Francisco; (415) 621-5570
Daily 6 - 10:45
Beer & wine
BA, MC
Reservations advisable

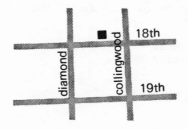

Mama's

If my mama cooked like this mama, I would
never have left home—probably because I couldn't
have wedged myself through the door. Mama's is
one of those places where you can inhale the
calories and then go crazy trying to decide what
to gorge yourself on. It's a little bitty place on a
corner across from Washington Square, and at first
glance it resembles an ice cream parlor. There are
only 13 or 14 tables and you have to wait in line to
order. While you stand there, you can watch the
talented ladies behind the counter create mouth-
watering masterpieces. And by the time it's your
turn to choose, you want one of each.

You can pick from super sandwiches, incredible
salads, fantastic "momelettes," French toast and
pancakes. While you can eat dinner here, your best
bet is brunch. The "momelettes," French toast
and pancakes are out of this world. Sandwiches
are made on your choice of bread: your own
baguette, rye, honey wheat, nut raisin, English muffin, Swedish cinnamon, onion or egg roll.

The pastries will threaten your sanity. Rather
than lose it, order strawberry shortcake (with
mountains of whipped cream and egg-sized strawberries) or pecan pie (the pecans seem the size of
beach balls). Or the custard torte or . . . even the
French toast is good enough to be dessert.

1701 Stockton St., San Francisco; (415) 362-6421
Daily 8 - 8
No bar
No credit cards
No reservations taken

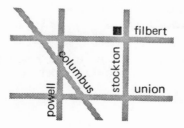

Tiffany's

Tiffany's is a jewel of a restaurant. Located on a corner in an unimpressive building, it rewards you with joyful surprises when you walk in. The room is two stories high with a balcony along two walls, lots of wood—staircase, tables, banisters, shingles and paneling—and Tiffany lamps. On a bright day, sunshine filters through the stained-glass windows and blends with the bright yellow ceiling.

The pizza here is the original Sicilian deep-dish version, and is really pizza *pie*. The crust is thick, yet it doesn't taste doughy or get soggy from all the good things put on top of it. Other specialties include spaghetti, ravioli, veal cutlet parmigiana, lasagne, cannelloni, seafood and steak. In addition, light, fluffy omelettes served with toast and pan-fried potatoes are available all day. Many other breakfasts, such as pancakes and sourdough French toast, plus a variety of sandwiches, are also offered. Obviously, the choice is vast.

We recommend that you try the pizza first (it usually takes 20 to 25 minutes to prepare) and then, if you have any stomach space left, one of the other gems on the menu.

1900 Market St., San Francisco; (415) 626-1309
Mon. - Thurs. 11 a.m. - 4 a.m.; Fri. & Sat. open
24 hours; Sun. closed at midnight
Beer & wine
No credit cards
No reservations taken

Note: This great place to eat has unfortunately burned down, but should reopen soon.

Victoria Station

Railroad trains have always seemed to be a symbol of the Old West, and detached boxcars seem to shelter the ghosts of decades of hoboes. Why is it, then, that a bunch of boxcars welded together and decorated with British and Australian railroad memen tos and relics seems like a foreign port? And why is it that prime rib served in this foreign atmosphere tastes perfect?

Whatever the secret, the management of Victoria Station has uncovered it and put it to good use in this restaurant by the embarcadero. Unfortunately, a great many people have discovered Victoria Station On Friday or Saturday night the wait for dinner can be as long as two hours. And no reservations are taken. So if you want to sample the outstanding beef prepared here, we suggest that you do it during the week. Prices are high, but the quality of meat served here explains that.

In addition to the outstanding meat, there is an exceptional salad bar from which you help yourself. And if you end up waiting at the bar (which could happen even during the week), you can stoke up on free cheese and crackers while imbibing some man-sized drinks.

50 Broadway at the Embarcadoro, San Francisco;
(415) 433-4400
Mon. - Thurs. 5:30 - 11; Fri. & Sat. 5 - midnight;
Sun. 5 - 10
Full bar
AE, BA, MC
No reservations taken

Mandarin

We knew there just had to·be a worthwhile restaurant in Ghirardelli Square, and this is it. If you enjoy Mandarin cooking, there is no better place to eat it than this gorgeous restaurant.

Once you decide to go, we suggest that you call a day in advance and order either the Mandarin duck (which serves four or more) or the smoked tea duck (also serving four or more); both dishes are superb, but require a day's notice to prepare. If you go on the spur of the moment, you can try the unusual combination dinners, which can include such delicacies as sweet and sour meatball Mandarin, green pepper chicken or shrimp a la Shanghai.

Aside from the incredible quality of the food, the atmosphere at the Mandarin really encourages your digestion. Beamed ceilings, lanterns and Chinese artifacts add splendor to the attractive interior, and the service is faultless. If you're lucky, Mr. Chien, the manager, will come to your table to explain how to eat a particular dish, what region it comes from and many other interesting details. You will want to return often.

Ghirardelli Square (2nd level of Woolen Mill Building,
   San Francisco; (415) 673-8812
Daily noon - 11:45
Full bar
AE, BA, CB, DC, MC
Reservations essential

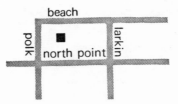

Chez Panisse

Dining at Chez Panisse is like *table d'hote* dining in a small French hotel during tourist season. In other words, you eat in the dining room of a home that has been converted to a restaurant, and there is a set menu each day at a fixed price. The house has been given a very attractive new facade, and the interior is charming—very much like that hotel dining room in your imagination.

The best way to describe the delicious food is to tell you what the menus were for two days during a recent week. Day 1: warm spinach salad with bacon and croutons; puree of carrots with white wine, served with a Madeira cream garnish; chicken braised in shallots and champagne with mushrooms and cream sauce (or veal sweetbreads prepared the same way); salad or cheese; fruit; and coffee or tea ($6.50). Day 2: avocado salad with fresh mayonnaise; cream fish soup with shrimp, Normandy style; fresh trout poached in court bouillon and white wine, served in a brioche with mushrooms, rice, shallots, tarragon and eggs: and the two last courses previously mentioned ($7.50).

Dinner menus for the week may be picked up each Tuesday, and lunch and Sunday brunch are also served. Any meal is a delight here.

1517 Shattuck Ave., Berkeley; (415) 548-5525
Daily, lunch: 11:30 - 2, dinner: 6 - 9
Beer & wine
No credit cards
Reservations essential

Le Beaujolais

Luckily, the waiters at Le Beaujolais are extremely helpful. Otherwise, you'd have to bring a French dictionary just to understand the menu. Actually, the most important thing to understand is that even if you ordered without knowing what you were pointing to, any dish you picked would be terrific.

Entrees range from salmon to rabbit to duckling to veal to steak, and great care is taken in their preparation. Dinners include either onion soup or soup of the day (our cream of celery was smooth and flavorful), a dinner salad served after the entree, and hot, crisp French bread. The vegetables served with the rabbit were rather dull and seemed to be there more for decoration than for additional culinary enjoyment—our only disappointment. The rabbit (actually *le lapin a la dijonnaise*), on the other hand, was superb. The escargot appetizers were also excellent—tender, well seasoned and bubbling hot.

If you're undecided, ask the waiter to make a suggestion. We did this and found everything he recommended to be delightful.

2415 Clement St., San Francisco; (415) 752-3921
Wed. - Sun. 5:30 - 10:30; closed Mon. & Tues.
Wine only
No credit cards
Reservations advisable

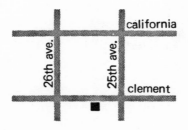

Le Petit

It is really difficult to classify Le Petit as a "splurge" restaurant when you consider the quality and quantity of food you get within a price range of $5.50 to $7. The only French-Swiss restaurant in San Francisco will serve you, for the price of dinner, pate maison, cream of spinach soup, green salad with homemade dressing, your choice from about six entrees, a dessert of parfait liqueur, tea or Sanka and all the house wine you can drink.

On our last visit, the entrees included omelette champagne (stuffed with French sausage and mushrooms in a light tomato-based sauce), truite a l'estrag (boneless trout with tarragon sauce), coq au vin Francois (boneless half-chicken simmered in wine and herbs), shrimps delicieux (tiny bay shrimps in egg and sherry sauce) and beef and lobster stew (beef stew with baby lobster tail, zucchini, bell pepper, eggplant, tomato, etc.). And each course was delightful. We especially enjoyed the cream of spinach soup the omelette champagne and the light, ice-creamy dessert.

Service here is excellent, but you'd better allow close to two hours for the full meal. The atmosphere is candle-lit and intimate, yet the decor is simple. Le Petit is truly a place to enjoy a fine meal.

381 South Van Ness Ave., San Francisco; (415) 861-2586
Tues. - Sun. 6 - 10; closed Mon.
Wine only
No credit cards
Reservations advisable

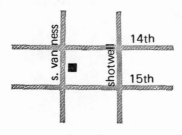

Paprika

You want to impress somebody and do yourself a favor at the same time? Drive to serene Mill Valley and treat yourself to dinner at the Paprika. There simply aren't any adequate adjectives to describe the fine food served in this quaint restaurant. That could be because the food is so Viennese that only one of those 25-letter German words would do it justice.

Dinners, which include soup, salad, entree and coffee, run slightly above $5. Some of the finer selections are rahmschnitzel (veal with dumplings and fried eggplant), Innsbruck geschnetzeltes (finger-sliced veal with special sauce, served with garden vegetables and dumplings) and Salzburger klops (sliced beef and veal in a patty shell with caper-and-horseradish sauce, served with roast potatoes and fresh vegetables).

The restaurant is decorated with floral tablecloths, print wallpaper, shingles on the walls and shutters on the windows, and it sits in the shade of a big tree. The total effect is charming, and very reminiscent of old Vienna—even if you've never been there. Service is friendly, and light classical music plays while you dine. The owner, Steven Wiley, was formerly with Trader Vic, and he has obviously gotten off to a good start in trying to match the reputation of that famous San Francisco restaurant.

52 Throckmorton, Mill Valley; (415) 388-8059
Wed. - Sat. 6 - 10; Sun. 5 - 10; closed Tues.
Beer & wine
BA, MC
Reservations advisable

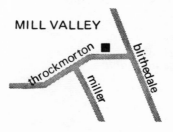

MILL VALLEY

Taj Majal

If you enjoy a good curry, or if you've never tasted a good curry and would like to try one, treat yourself to dinner at the Taj Mahal.

While a complete sampling of the offerings could escalate your bill to "splurge" level, the *a la carte* curries are very reasonable. (The complete dinners include soup, rice, lentils, condiments, bread, tea or coffee and dessert.) There is also an enticing variety of special mixed drinks, including the Maharaja Bombshell, which has a champagne base with some top-secret tingle ingredients added.

Of the dinners we tried, we definitely thought the chicken dishes the best—muglai chicken, chicken tandoori and the house special, chicken a la taj. The differences in their preparation are subtle and done basically with spices. The lamb and the pork were also good, but less distinctive than the chicken.

The Taj Mahal is a small, dimly lit restaurant that seems to overheat on occasion. The decor is simple, with framed batiks on the walls and about 13 cloth-covered tables. Service here is attentive; your host will even read your tea leaves upon reques While the curries are not overly spicy, they are exceptionally flavorful and can be enjoyed as an introduction to or confirmation of the delights of Indian food.

314 Columbus Ave. at Braodway; San Francisco; (415) 398-3555
Daily, lunch 11:30 - 2:30; dinner 5:30 - 10:30
Beer & wine
AE, BA, CB, MC
Reservations advisable

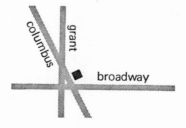

Mingei-Ya

The traditions of the Orient always seem mysterious because they're so different from those of Western cultures. Many people probably even have secret ambitions to be samurai warriors or to have someone tiptoe over their vertebrae. Since these experiences are out of reach for most of us, we have to experience Oriental culture as it is translated locally.

One of the best places to do this is Mingei-Ya. Here you dine Japanese country-style, sitting on mats on the floor at low tables. You are required to check your shoes at the door (better remember to darn those socks) and wear paper sandals, which are given to you to keep. While you dine in open rooms, the atmosphere is private and the service attentive and personal.

Several dinners are available, including the specialty dinner of Mingei-Ya, o-mizu-taki: prime rib beef ribbons with vegetables, mushrooms and bean cake, flavored with a special sauce, served with rice and prepared in a copper stove at your table. Superb.

Sukiyaki, teriyaki, tempura and sashimi dinners are also available. Dinners include hors d'oeuvres, soup, Japanese pickled tidbits, tea and dessert.

2033 Union St., San Francisco; (415) 567-2553
Tues. - Sun. 5 - 10; closed Mon.
Beer & wine
AE, BA, MC
Reservations essential

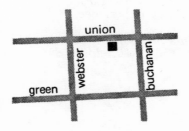

Bali's

Bali's is a restaurant that has to be recommended, because it definitely does not have the kind of enticing facade that advertises what is happening within. In fact, from the outside, Bali's looks like part of any old office building in San Francisco's financial district.

But once you walk inside, the mood envelops you. The darkness in the small, dimly lit dining room is punctuated only by the stacks of Armenian bread sitting like crisp white ruffles in baskets on the immaculately set tables.

There are only three dinners: shish kebab, special shish kebab and rack of lamb. The complete dinner is about $7 per person. But if you've ever hungered for tender, succulent lamb, you would be doing you a disservice by not dining in this elegant oasis.

Dinner begins with cold, crunchy vegetables and Armenian bread and cheese. This is all on the table and you help yourself. Then a beautiful salad with a light, spicy house dressing is served by the tuxedoe waiters. Then comes the entree, and we highly recom mend the rack of lamb. It is cook in pomegranate juice and the flavor is indescribable. It is served im peccably with mounds of rice pilaf, a broiled tomato and a crab apple. For dessert, try the baklava. You will enjoy its lightness and delicate sweetness.

If you've been meaning to go someplace special, yet unusual, try Bali's. Eating there will be a re warding culinary experience.

615 Sansome St., San Francisco; (415) 982-5059
Tues. - Sat. 6:30 - 10; closed Sun. & Mon.
Full bar
AE, MC
Reservations advisable

Bali

Mamounia's

Dining at Mamounia's is one of the most exciting and fulfilling gastronomic experiences you may ever have.

Once inside, you are immediately transported to a Moroccan world, complete with plush pillows, billowing canopies, low tables—and no silverware. Unless you were raised by a Moroccan mommy, you probably were encouraged to repress any urge to stick your fingers in your food. At Mamounia's, it is expected that this is the way you will dine. Water is even poured over your hands before you begin to eat.

Dinners are priced from about $8 to $9 and each one is truly a feast. All dinners include salad, soup, bastilla (a light, flaky, pie-like affair filled with chicken and incredible spices), entree, pastry and tea. And each course seems to surpass the previous one. The salad here is a combination of cooked vegetables which you spoon up with a piece of bread. The lamb soup is rich with pureed vegetables and more spices. The entrees include such delights as lamb with prunes (or honey) and chicken with lemon. The pastry is sweet and crispy.

If you're in the mood to splurge and really get carried away, and if you want to experience a dinner over which you will become unabashedly enthusiastic, Mamounia's is a must.

4411 Balboa St. at 45th Ave., San Francisco;
(415) 752-6566
Mon. - Sat. 5 - 11; closed Sun.
Beer & wine
MC
Reservations advisable

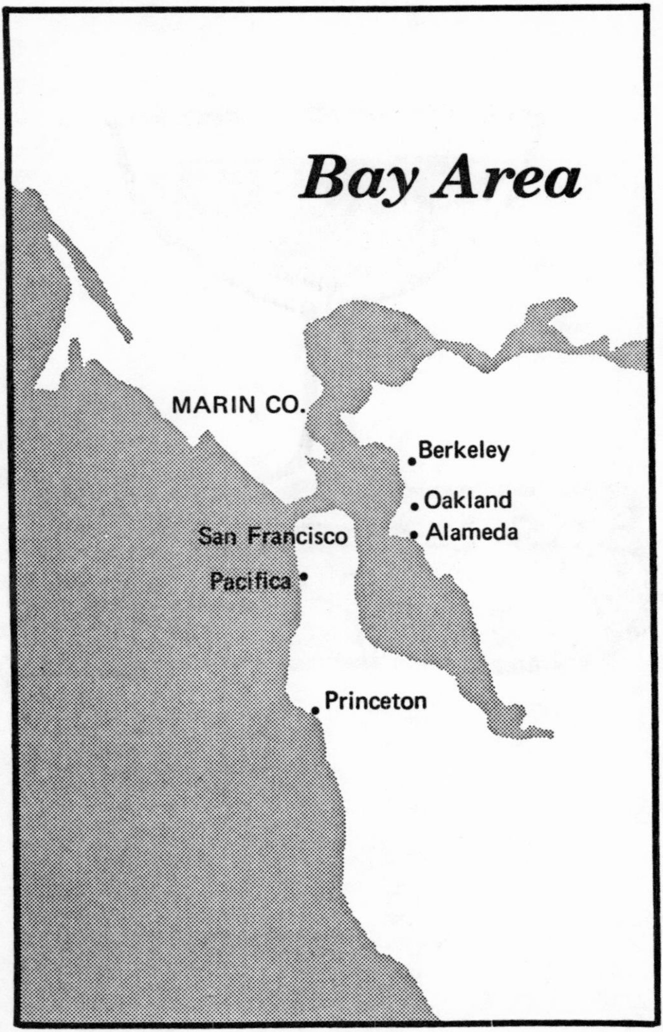

Bay Area

MARIN CO.

San Francisco

Pacifica

• Berkeley

• Oakland
• Alameda

• Princeton

Area Index

Alphabetical Index

216

Camaro Publishing Co.
Newwest ®

A Special Notice to our readers:

Excellence is our publishing aim—to provide the best, most accurate and timely information in the world about travel/adventure, good food and wine, all at the very lowest prices. We have discovered that you don't have to spend a fortune to enjoy dining out or travel. You just have to know where to go.

To speed making our latest information available to the adventurous, we have just started the Newwest California Club which will present monthly, the very latest of the very best. . .and all for not much money. Try it and see.

Newwest California Club Membership

Mail To: Secretary, Newwest California Club
P.O. Box 90430, Los Angeles, Ca., 90009

$3.00 per year or special charter subscription:
$6.00 for three years, or $25 for lifetime
Gold Circle membership.

Membership includes subscription to NEWWEST.

New Member:

Name _____

Street _____

City, State, Zip _____

Enclosed $ _____

Other ❤ Camaro Guides

All beautifully illustrated with maps and sketches

. . . For your low cost dining pleasure, plus a few splurges.

☐ Hidden Restaurants: Northern California
☐ Hidden Restaurants: Southern California
☐ Little Restaurants of Los Angeles
☐ Little Restaurants of San Francisco
☐ Little Restaurants of San Diego

. . . Or for just a bit of adventure throughout the
California Countryside.

☐ Wine Tasting in California: A Free Weekend
☐ L.A. On Foot: A Free Afternoon

TO: Camaro Publishing Co.
   P. O. Box 90430
   Los Angeles, California 90009

Please send the books checked above. Enclosed is $ _____
which includes $1.95 per book ordered, plus 6% tax and
25¢ postage/handling.

Name _____

Address _____

City _____ State _____ Zip _____ _

☐ Check here to include your name on the mailing list
for new announcements of Camaro's Adventure Guides.

☐ California Wine Tasting Calendar. $3.00 plus tax and
25¢ postage/handling.

FREE Dinner for Two

If you think we've made some blatant omissions in our selections, please send us the name of your favorite restaurant not mentioned in a Camaro Guide. Every other month we'll draw a card, you could win a free dinner for two at a restaurant in your area of California. It's worth a try, just tear out this postcard and drop it in the mail.

Name of Restaurant: _____

Address: _____

Phone #: _____

Type of food served: _____

_____

Price range for dinners: _____

Your favorite dish: _____

_____

Other comments: _____

_____

Your name: _____

Your address: _____

_____

Any comments on the book: _____

_____

CAMARO PUBLISHING COMPANY
477½ Vallejo Street
San Francisco, California 94133